ESSENTIALS

IN

CONDUCTING

BY

KARL WILSON GEHRKENS

PROFESSOR OF SCHOOL MUSIC
OBERLIN CONSERVATORY OF MUSIC

AUTHOR OF "MUSIC NOTATION AND TERMINOLOGY,"
"FUNDAMENTALS OF MUSIC,"
"HANDBOOK OF MUSICAL TERMS," ETC.

$1.75

OLIVER DITSON COMPANY

THEODORE PRESSER CO., DISTRIBUTORS
1712 Chestnut Street, Philadelphia

MADE IN U. S. A.

To the Memory of
ROBERT C. BEDFORD
for many years

SECRFTARY OF THE BOARD OF TRUSTEES
of
TUSKEGEE INSTITUTE

CONTENTS

PREFACE

In putting out this little book, the author is well aware of the fact that many musicians feel that conductors, like poets and teachers, are "born and not made"; but his experience in training supervisors of music has led him to feel that, although only the elementary phases of conducting can be taught, such instruction is nevertheless quite worth while, and is often surprisingly effective in its results. He has also come to believe that even the musical genius may profit by the experience of others and may thus be enabled to do effective work as a conductor more quickly than if he relied wholly upon his native ability.

The book is of course planned especially with the amateur in view, and the author, in writing it, has had in mind his own fruitless search for information upon the subject of conducting when he was just beginning his career as a teacher; and he has tried to say to the amateur of today those things that he himself so sorely needed to know at that time, and had to find out by blundering experience.

It should perhaps be stated that although the writer has himself had considerable experience in conducting, the material here presented is rather the result of observing and analyzing the work of others than an account of his own methods. In preparation for his task, the author has observed many of the better-known conductors in this country, both in rehearsal and in public performance, during a period of some twelve years, and the book represents an attempt to put into simple language and practical form the ideas gathered from this observation.   It is hoped that as a result of reading these pages the amateur may not only have become more fully informed concerning those practical phases of conducting about which he has probably been seeking light, but may be inspired to further reading and additional music study in preparation for the larger aspects of the work.

The writer wishes to acknowledge the material assistance rendered him by Professor John Ross Frampton, of the Iowa State Teachers College, and Professor Osbourne McConathy, of Northwestern University, both of whom have read the book in manuscript and have given invaluable suggestions.   He wishes also to acknowledge his very large debt to Professor George Dickinson, of Vassar College, who has read the material both in manuscript and in proof, and to whose pointed comments and criticisms many improvements both in material and in arrangement are due.

K. W. G.

Oberlin, Ohio
  June, 1918

Essentials in Conducting

CHAPTER I – VII

INTRODUCTION

DEFINITION The word "conducting" as used in a musical sense now ordinarily refers to the activities of an orchestra or chorus leader who stands before a group of performers and gives his entire time and effort to directing their playing or singing, to the end that a musically effective ensemble performance may result.

This is accomplished by means of certain conventional movements of a slender stick called a *baton* (usually held in the right hand), as well as through such changes of facial expression, bodily posture, *et cetera*, as will convey to the singers or players the conductor's wishes concerning the rendition of the music.

Conducting in this sense involves the responsibility of having the music performed at the correct tempo, with appropriate dynamic effects, with precise attacks and releases, and in a fitting spirit. This in turn implies that many details have been worked out in rehearsal, these including such items as making certain that all performers sing or play the correct tones in the correct rhythm; insisting upon accurate pronunciation and skilful enunciation of the words in vocal music; indicating logical and musical phrasing; correcting mistakes in breathing or bowing; and, in general, stimulating orchestra or chorus to produce a tasteful rendition of the music as well as an absolutely perfect *ensemble* with all parts in correct proportion and perfect balance.

In order to have his directing at the public performance function properly, it thus becomes the conductor's task to plan and to administer the rehearsals in such a way that the performers may become thoroughly familiar with the music, both in technique and in spirit. In other words, the conductor must play the part of musical manager as well as that of artistic inspirer, and if he does not perform his task in such fashion as to be looked up to by the members of his chorus or orchestra as the real leader, and if he himself does not feel confident of being able to do his work better than any one else upon the ground, he cannot possibly be successful in any very high degree. A conductor must first of all be a strong leader, and failing in this, no amount of musical ability or anything else will enable him to conduct well. We shall have more to say upon this point in a later chapter.

SUMMARY OF THE HISTORY OF CONDUCTING Conducting of one kind or another has undoubtedly been practised for many centuries, but directing by gestures of the hand has not been traced farther back than the fourteenth century, at which time Heinrich von Meissen, a Minnesinger, is represented in an old manuscript directing a group of musicians with stick in hand. In the fifteenth century the leader of the Sistine Choir at Rome directed the singers with a roll of paper (called a "sol-fa"), held in his hand. By the latter part of the seventeenth century it had become customary for the conductor to sit at the harpsichord or organ, filling in the harmonies from a "figured bass," and giving any needed signals with one hand or the head as best he could. Conducting during this period signified merely keeping the performers together; that is, the chief function of the conductor was that of "time beater." With the advent of the conductor in the rôle of interpreter, such directing became obsolete, and from the early nineteenth century, and particularly as the result of the impetus given the art by the conducting of Mendelssohn, Berlioz, Liszt, and Wagner, the conductor has become an exceedingly important functionary, in these modern days even ranking with the *prima donna* in operatic performances! It is now the conductor's aim not merely to see that a composition is played correctly and with good ensemble; more than that, the leader of today gives his own version or *reading* of the composition just as the pianist or violinist does. Instead of being a mere "time beater" he has become an interpreter, and (except in the case of the organist-director of a choir) he attempts to do nothing except so to manipulate his musical forces as to secure an effective performance.

THE PSYCHOLOGICAL BASIS OF CONDUCTING   The conductor works largely through the instrumentality of *instinctive imitation;* that is, his methods are founded upon the fact that human beings have an innate tendency to copy the actions of others, often without being conscious that they are doing so. Thus, if one person yawns or coughs, a second person observing him has an instinctive tendency to do likewise. One member of a group is radiant with happiness, and very soon the others catch the infection and are smiling also; a singer at a public performance strains to get a high tone, and instinctively our faces pucker up and our throat muscles become tense, in sympathetic but entirely unconscious imitation. In very much the same way in conducting, the leader sets the tempo,— and is imitated by the musicians under him; he feels a certain emotional thrill in response to the composer's message,—and arouses a similar thrill in the performers; lifts his shoulders as though taking breath,—and causes the singers to phrase properly, often without either the conductor or the singers being aware of how the direction was conveyed.   It is at least partly because we instinctively imitate the mental state or the emotional attitude of the pianist or the vocalist that we are capable of being thrilled or calmed by musical performances, and it is largely for this reason that an audience always insists upon *seeing* the artist as well as hearing him.   In the same way the musicians in a chorus or orchestra must see the conductor and catch from him by instinctive imitation his attitude toward the music being performed. This point will be more fully discussed in a later chapter, when we take up interpretation in conducting.

CONDUCTING
A COMBINATION OF
SCIENCE AND ART
In setting out to become a conductor it will be well for the young musician to recognize at the outset that by far the larger part of the conductor's work rests upon an art basis, and that only a comparatively small portion of it is science; hence he must not expect to find complete information concerning his future work in any treatise upon the subject.   It is one thing to state that there are three primary colors, or that orange is the result of mixing red and yellow, but it is a very different matter to give directions for painting an effective landscape, or a true-to-life portrait.   One thing involves *science* only, but the other is concerned primarily with *art*, and it is always dangerous to dogmatize concerning matters artistic.   To carry the illustration one step farther, we may say that it is comparatively easy to teach a pupil to strike certain piano keys in such a way as to produce the correct melody, harmony, and rhythm of a certain composition; but who would venture, even in these days of frenzied advertising, to promise that in so many lessons he could teach a pupil to play it as a Hofmann or a Paderewski would?   Here again we see clearly the contrast between science and art, matters of

science being always susceptible of organization into a body of principles and laws *which will work in every case*, while art is intangible, subtle, and ever-varying.

The application of our illustration to conducting should now be clear. We may teach a beginner how to wield a baton according to conventional practice, how to secure firm attacks and prompt releases, and possibly a few other definitely established facts about conducting; but unless our would-be leader has musical feeling within him and musicianship back of him, it will be utterly futile for him to peruse these pages further, or to make any other kind of an attempt to learn to conduct; for, as stated above, only a very small part of conducting can be codified into rules, directions, and formulæ, by far the larger part of our task being based upon each individual's own innate musical feeling, and upon the general musical training that he has undergone. All this may be discouraging, but on the other hand, granting a fair degree of native musical ability, coupled with a large amount of solid music study, any one possessing a sense of leadership can, after a reasonable amount of intelligent practice, learn to handle a chorus or even an orchestra in a fairly satisfactory manner. It is our purpose in general to treat the scientific rather than the artistic side of conducting, and we are taking for granted, therefore, that the reader is endowed with musical feeling at least in a fair degree, and has acquired the rudiments of musical scholarship as the result of an extensive study of piano, organ, singing, ear-training, music history, harmony, *et cetera*, and especially by attentive listening to a very large amount of good music with score in hand. As a result of combining such musical ability with a careful reading of these pages and with a large amount of practice in actually wielding the baton, it is hoped that the beginner will arrive at his goal somewhat earlier than he would if he depended entirely upon what the psychologist calls the "trial-and-error" method of learning.

IMPORTANCE OF MUSICAL SCHOLARSHIP　The musical amateur who is ambitious to conduct should therefore study music in all its phases, and if in doubt as to his talent, he should submit to a vocational test in order to determine whether his native musical endowment is sufficient to make it worth his while to study the art seriously. If the result of the test is encouraging, showing a good ear, a strong rhythmic reaction, and a considerable amount of what might be termed native musical taste, let him practise his piano energetically and intelligently, and especially let him learn to read three and four voices on separate staffs (as in a vocal score) in order to prepare himself for future reading of full scores. Let him study harmony, counterpoint, form, and, if possible, composition and orchestration. Let him work indefatigably at ear-training, and particularly at harmonic ear training, so that notes and tones may become closely associated in his mind, the printed page then giving him auditory rather than merely visual imagery; in other words, let him school himself to make the printed page convey to his mind the actual sounds of the music. Let him study the history of music, not only as a record of the work of individual composers, but as an account of what has transpired in the various periods or epochs of musical art, so that he may become intelligent concerning the ideals, the styles, and the forms of these various periods. And finally, let him hear all the good music he possibly can, listening to it from the threefold standpoint of sense, emotion, and intellect, and noting particularly those matters connected with expression and interpretation in these renditions. In as many cases as possible let him study the scores of the compositions beforehand, comparing then his own ideas of interpretation with those of the performer or conductor, and formulating reasons for any differences of opinion that may become manifest.

Let the young musician also form the habit of reading

widely, not only along all musical lines (history, biography, theory, esthetics, *et cetera*), but upon a wide variety of topics, such as painting and the other arts, history, literature, sociology, pedagogy, *et cetera*. As the result of such study and such reading, a type of musical scholarship will be attained which will give the conductor an authority in his interpretations and criticisms that cannot possibly be achieved in any other way. Let us hasten to admit at once that the acquiring of this sort of scholarship will take a long time, and that it cannot all be done before beginning to conduct. But in the course of several years of broad and intelligent study a beginning at least can be made, and later on, as the result of continuous growth while at work, a fine, solid, comprehensive scholarship may finally eventuate.

CHAPTER II

Personal Traits Necessary in Conducting

IMPORTANCE OF PERSONALITY In the introductory chapter it was noted that the conductor must build upon a foundation of musical scholarship if he is to be really successful; that he must possess musical feeling; and that he must go through extensive musical training, if he is to conduct with taste and authority. But in addition to these purely *musical* requirements, experience and observation have demonstrated that the would-be conductor must be possessed of certain definitely established personal characteristics, and that many a musician who has been amply able to pass muster from a musical standpoint, has failed as a conductor because he lacked these other traits.

It is not my purpose to give at this point an exhaustive list of qualities that must form the personal equipment of the conductor. In general it will be sufficient to state that he must possess in a fair degree those personal traits that are advantageous in any profession. But of these desirable qualities three or four seem to be so indispensable that it has been thought best to devote a brief chapter to a discussion of them. These qualities are:

1. A sense of humor.
2. A creative imagination.
3. A sense of leadership combined with organizing ability.

A SENSE OF HUMOR The first of these traits, a sense of humor, may perhaps upon first thought seem a peculiar quality to include in a category of virtues for the professional man of any type, and especially for the musician. But upon reflection it will be admitted that the ability to see things in a humorous light (which very frequently means merely seeing them in true perspective) has helped many a man to avoid wasting nervous energy upon insignificant occurrences, while the lack of this ability has caused more trouble among all sorts of people (and particularly, it seems to me, among musicians) than any other single thing.

ILLUSTRATIONS
OF HUMOR IN
THE REHEARSAL
Some player or singer is either overarduous or a bit sleepy during the first stages of rehearsing a new composition, and makes a wrong entrance, perhaps during a pause just before the climacteric point. The occurrence is really funny and the other performers are inclined to smile or snicker, but our serious conductor quells the outbreak with a scowl. The humorous leader, on the other hand, sees the occurrence as the performers do, joins in the laugh that is raised at the expense of the offender, and the rehearsal goes on with renewed spirit.

An instrumental performer makes a bad tone, and the conductor laughs at him, saying it sounds like a wolf howling or an ass braying. If the remark is accompanied by a smile, the performer straightens up and tries to overcome the fault; but if the comment is made with a snarl there is a tightening up of muscles, an increased tension of the nerves, and the performer is more than likely to do worse the next time.

There is a difference of opinion between the conductor and some performer about fingering or bowing, phrasing or interpretation, and a quarrel seems imminent; but the conductor refuses to take the matter too seriously, and, having ample authority for his own viewpoint, proceeds as he has begun, later on talking it over with the performer, and perhaps giving him a reason for his opinion.

Humor is thus seen to have the same effect upon a body of musicians as oil applied to machinery, and musical machinery seems to need more of this kind of lubrication than almost any other variety.

But the conductor must distinguish carefully between sarcastic wit, which laughs *at*, and humor, which laughs *with*. In a book bearing the copyright date of 1849, the writer distinguishes between the two, in the following words:*

> Humor originally meant moisture, a signification it metaphorically retains, for it is the very juice of the mind, enriching and fertilizing where it falls. Wit laughs at; humor laughs with. Wit lashes external appearances, or cunningly exchanges single foibles into character; humor glides into the heart of its object, looks lovingly upon the infirmities it attacks, and represents the whole man. Wit is abrupt, scornful . . . ; humor is slow and shy, insinuating its fun into your heart.

THE VALUE OF A CHEERFUL ATTITUDE   The conductor with a sense of humor will ordinarily have the advantage also of being cheerful in his attitude toward the performers, and this is an asset of no mean significance. It is a well-known psychophysical fact that the human body does much better work when the mind is free from care, and that in any profession or vocation, other things being equal, the worker who is cheerful and optimistic will perform his labor much more efficiently at the expense of considerably less mental and bodily energy than he who is ill-humored, worried, fretful, and unable to take a joke. But the *foreman* who possesses this quality of cheerfulness and humor is doubly fortunate, for he not only secures the beneficial results in his own case, but by suggestion frequently arouses the same desirable state of mind and body in those who are working under him. It is particularly because of this latter fact that the conductor needs to cultivate a cheerful, even a humorous outlook, especially in the rehearsal. As the result of forming this habit, he will be enabled to give directions

* Whipple, *Literature and Life*, p. 91

in such a way that they will be obeyed cheerfully (and consequently more effectively); he will find it possible to rehearse longer with less fatigue both to himself and to his musical forces; and he will be able to digest his food and to sleep soundly after the rehearsal because he is not worrying over trivial annoyances that, after all, should have been dismissed with a laugh as soon as they appeared. There must not of course be so much levity that the effectiveness of the rehearsal will be endangered, but there is not much likelihood that this will happen; whereas there seems to be considerable danger that our rehearsals will become too cold and formal. A writer on the psychology of laughter states that "laughter is man's best friend";* and in another place (p. 342) says that the smile always brings to the mind "relaxation from strain."

THE VALUE OF IMAGINATION IN CONDUCTING Creative imagination is an inborn quality—"a gift of the gods"—and if the individual does not possess it, very little can be done for him in the artistic realm. Constructive or creative imagination implies the ability to combine known elements in new ways—*to use the mind forwards,* as it were. The possession of this trait makes it possible to picture to oneself how things are going to look or sound or feel before any actual sense experience has taken place; to see into people's minds and often find out in advance how they are going to react to a projected situation; to combine chemical elements in new ways and thus create new substances; to plan details of organization in a manufacturing establishment or in an educational institution, and to be able to forecast how these things are going to work out.

It is this quality of creative imagination that enables the inventor to project his mind into the future and see a continent spanned by railways and telephones,

* Sully, *An Essay on Laughter.*

and the barrier of an ocean broken down by means of wireless and aeroplane; and in every case the inventor works with old and well-known materials, being merely enabled by the power of his creative faculties (as they are erroneously called) to combine these known materials in new ways.

In the case of the musician, such creative imagination has always been recognized as a *sine qua non* of original composition, but its necessity has not always been so clearly felt in the case of the performer. Upon analyzing the situation it becomes evident, however, that the performer cannot possibly get from the composer his real message unless he can follow him in his imagination, and thus re-create the work. As for adding anything original to what the composer has given, this is plainly out of the question unless the interpreter is endowed somewhat extensively with creative imagination; and the possession of this quality will enable him to introduce such subtle variations from a cut-and-dried, merely *accurate* rendition as will make his performance seem really spontaneous, and will inevitably arouse a more enthusiastic emotional response in the listeners.

Weingartner sums up the value of imagination in the final paragraph of one of the few really valuable books on conducting at our disposal.*

More and more I have come to think that what decides the worth of conducting is the degree of suggestive power that the conductor can exercise over the performers. At the rehearsals he is mostly nothing more than a workman, who schools the men under him so conscientiously and precisely that each of them knows his place and what he has to do there; he first becomes an artist when the moment comes for the production of the work. Not even the most assiduous rehearsing, so necessary a prerequisite as this is, can so stimulate the capacities of the players as the force of imagination of the conductor. It is not the transference of his personal will, but the mysterious act of creation that called the work itself into being takes place again in him, and transcending the narrow limits of reproduction, he becomes a new-creator, a self-creator.

* Weingartner, *On Conducting*, translated by Ernest Newman, p. 56.

This quality is indispensable to all musicians, be they creators or performers, but is especially desirable in the conductor, for he needs it not only from the standpoint of interpretation, as already noted, but from that of manager or organizer. Upon this latter point we shall have more to say later, but it may be well to state just here that if the conductor could imagine what was going on in the minds of his players or singers, and could see things from their viewpoint; if he could forecast the effect of his explanatory directions or of his disciplinary rulings, nine-tenths of all the quarreling, bickering, and general dissatisfaction that so frequently mar the work of any musical organization could easily be eliminated. We might also add that if the conductor could only foresee the effect upon his audiences of certain works, or of certain interpretations, his plans would probably often be materially altered.

ORGANIZING ABILITY AND A SENSE OF LEADERSHIP But the conductor must be more than a humorous-minded and imaginative musician. He must also (especially in these modern times) be an organizer, a business man, a leader. The qualities of leadership and organizing ability are so closely connected that we shall for the most part treat them together in our discussion, and they are so important that a fairly extensive analysis will be attempted.

In an article on Schumann in *Grove's Dictionary* Dr. Philip Spitta, the well-known historian and critic, comments upon the conducting of this famous composer as follows:*

Schumann was sadly wanting in the real talent for conducting. All who ever saw him conduct or played under his direction are agreed on this point. Irrespective of the fact that conducting for any length of time tired him out, he had neither the collectedness and prompt presence of mind, nor the sympathetic faculty, nor the enterprising dash, without each of which conducting

* *Grove's Dictionary of Music and Musicians*, New Edition, Vol. IV, p. 363.

in the true sense is impossible.   He even found difficulty in starting at a given tempo; nay, he even sometimes shrank from giving any initial beat, so that some energetic pioneer would begin without waiting for the signal, and without incurring Schumann's wrath!   Besides this, any thorough practice, bit by bit, with his orchestra, with instructive remarks by the way as to the mode of execution, was impossible to this great artist, who in this respect was a striking contrast to Mendelssohn.   He would have a piece played through, and if it did not answer to his wishes, have it repeated.   If it went no better the second or perhaps third time, he would be extremely angry at what he considered the clumsiness, or even the ill-will of the players; but detailed remarks he never made.

This estimate of Schumann's work as a conductor demonstrates unmistakably that he failed in this particular field, not because his musical scholarship was not adequate, but because he did not have that peculiar ability which enables one man to dominate others: *viz.*, *a sense of leadership*, or *personal magnetism*, as it is often called.   Seidl asserts* that Berlioz, Massenet, and Saint-Saëns likewise failed as conductors, in spite of recognized musicianship; and it is of course well known that even Beethoven and Brahms could not conduct their own works as well as some of their contemporaries whose names are now almost forgotten.

The feeling that one has the power to cause others to do one's will seems in most cases to be inborn, at least certain children display it at a very early age; and it is usually the boys and girls who decide on the playground what games shall be played next, or what mischief shall now be entered upon, who later on become leaders in their several fields of activity.   And yet this sense of leadership, or something closely approximating it, may also be acquired, at least to a certain extent, by almost any one who makes a consistent and intelligent attempt in this direction.   It is this latter fact which may encourage those of us who are not naturally as gifted along these lines as we should like to be, and it is because of this possibility of acquiring what in conducting amounts

* Seidl, *The Music of the Modern World*, Vol. I, p. 106.

to an indispensable qualification that an attempt is here made to analyze the thing called leadership into its elements.

THE FIRST ELEMENT IN LEADERSHIP The primary basis upon which a sense of leadership rests is undoubtedly confidence in one's general ability and in one's knowledge of the particular subject being handled. The leader must not only know but must know that he knows. This makes quick judgments possible, and the leader and organizer must always be capable of making such judgments, and of doing it with finality. The baseball player must decide instantly whether to throw the ball to "first," "second," "third," or "home," and he must repeatedly make such decisions correctly before he can become a strong and respected baseball captain. The same thing holds true of the foreman in a factory, and both baseball captain and factory foreman must not only know every detail of the work done under them, but must *know that they know it*, and must feel confident of being able to cause those working under them to carry it on as they conceive it. So the conductor must not only know music, but must have confidence in his ear, in his rhythmic precision, in his taste, in his judgment of tempo, in short, in his musical scholarship; and he must not only feel that he knows exactly what should be done in any given situation, but be confident that he can make his chorus or orchestra do it as he wishes. Think for instance of securing a firm attack on the first tone of such a song as the *Marseillaise*. It is an extremely difficult thing to do, and it would be utterly impossible to direct any one else exactly how to accomplish it; and yet, if the conductor knows exactly how it must sound, if he has an auditory image of it before the actual tones begin, and if he feels that when he begins to beat time the chorus will sing as he has heard them in imagination, then the expected result is almost certain to follow. But if he is uncertain or hesitant upon any of these points, he will as surely fail to get a good attack.

Such confidence in one's own ability as we have been describing usually results in the acquiring of what is called an easy manner,—self-possession,—in short, *poise*, and it is the possession of such a bearing that gives us confidence in the scholarship and ability of the leaders in any type of activity. But the influence of this type of manner cannot be permanent unless it rests upon a foundation of really solid knowledge or ability.

THE SECOND ELEMENT IN LEADERSHIP The second element included in leadership and organizing ability is the power to make oneself understood, that is, clearness of speech and of expression. This involves probably first of all, so far as conducting is concerned, a voice that can be easily heard, even in a fairly large room, and that carries with it the tone of authority. But it includes also a good command of language so that one's ideas may be expressed clearly, and one's commands given definitely. An important point to be noted in this connection is that the conductor must be able to exercise rigid self-control, so as not to become incoherent under stress of anger, emergencies, or other excitement.

THE THIRD ELEMENT IN LEADERSHIP The final element involved in leadership is a tremendous love of and respect for the thing that is being done. Napoleon became a great general because of his confidence in his own ability, and because of his very great enthusiasm for his work. Lincoln became one of the greatest statesmen of all times largely because of his earnestness, his extraordinary love and respect for the common people, and his unfaltering confidence in the justice of the cause for which the North was contending. Pestalozzi could never have become one of the world's most influential teachers if he had not felt that the thing he was trying to do was a big thing, a vital thing in the life of his country, and if he had not had a real love in his heart for his work among the ragged and untrained urchins whom he gathered about him.

And for the same reason it is clear that no one can become a strong and forceful conductor who does not have an overwhelming love of music in his heart. We may go farther and say that no conductor can give a really spirited reading of a musical composition if he does not feel genuinely enthusiastic over the work being performed, and that one reason for the sluggish response that musicians often make to the conductor's baton is the mediocrity of the music which they are being asked to perform. The conductor is not in sympathy with it (sometimes without realizing this himself), and there is consequently no virility in the playing or singing. The remedy for this state of affairs consists, first, in allowing only those who have some taste in the selection of music to conduct; and second, in inspiring all con-ductors to take much more time and much greater pains in deciding upon the works to be rehearsed. In direct-ing a choir one may examine a dozen cantatas, or twenty-five anthems, before one is found that is really distinctive. If one stops at the second or third, and thinks that although not very good yet it is possibly good enough, very probably the choir will be found to be sluggish and unresponsive, filled with what Coward calls "inertia."* But if one goes on looking over more and more selections until something really distinctive is dis-covered, it is more than probable that the chorus will respond with energy and enthusiasm.

We have heard many arguments in favor of teaching children only the best music, and here is yet another, perhaps more potent than all the rest. They must be

---

* Coward, *Choral Technique and Interpretation*, p. 73.

taught only good music because you as a musician will find it impossible to become enthusiastic over mediocre or poor works; and if you do not yourself glow over the music that you are directing, you will hardly succeed in arousing the children's interest, for enthusiasm spreads by contagion, and there can be no spreading by contact unless we have a point from which to start.

A sense of leadership consists, then, of a combination of self-confidence and poise, clearness of speech and expression, and enthusiasm for one's work; and if with these three there is mingled the ability to think clearly and definitely, we have a combination that is bound to produce distinctive results, no matter what the field of activity may be. Let us repeat that the encouraging thing about the whole matter is the fact that most of the things involved in leadership can be *acquired*, at least to a certain degree, if persistent efforts are made for a long enough time.

Before going on with the topic to be treated in the next chapter, let us summarize the materials out of which our conductor is to be fashioned. They are:

1. Innate musical ability.
2. A long period of broad and intelligent music study.
3. An attractive and forceful personality.
4. A sense of humor.
5. A creative imagination.
6. Magnetic leadership and organizing ability.

Some of these qualities are admittedly almost diametrically opposed to one another, and it is probably because so few individuals combine such apparently opposite traits that such a small number of musicians succeed as conductors, and so few organizers and business men succeed as musicians. But in spite of this difficulty, we must insist again that any really tangible and permanent success in conducting involves a combination of these attributes, and that the conductor of the future, even more than of the past, must possess not only those qualities of the artist needed by the solo performer, but must in addition be a good business manager, an organizer, a tactician, a diplomat, a task-master—in plain English, a good *boss*. It is primarily because of the lack of these last-mentioned qualities that most musicians fail as conductors. A writer in the *Canadian Journal of Music*, signing himself Varasdin, sums it up well in the following words:

He who wishes to "carry away" his body of players as well as his audience, the former to a unanimously acted improvisation, the latter to a unanimously felt emotion, needs above all "commanding personal magnetism," and everything else must be subordinate to that.

He must be "very much alive"—(highly accumulated vital energy, always ready to discharge, is the secret of all personal magnetism)—and the alertness, the presence of mind, the acute and immediate perception of everything going on during rehearsal or performance, the dominancy and impressiveness of his minutest gesture, the absolute self-possession and repose even in working up the most exciting climaxes and in effecting the most sudden contrasts—all these are simply self-evident corollaries from our first and foremost requirement.

CHAPTER III

The Technique of the Baton

THE BATON
ITSELF
Before giving actual directions for the manipulation of the conductor's baton, it may be well to state that the stick itself should be light in weight, light in color, and from sixteen to twenty inches long. It must be thin and flexible, and should taper gradually from the end held in the hand to the point. Batons of this kind can be manufactured easily at any ordinary planing mill where there is a lathe. The kinds sold at stores are usually altogether too thick and too heavy. If at any time some adulating chorus or choir should present the conductor with an ebony baton with silver mountings, he must not feel that courtesy demands that it should be used in conducting. The proper thing to do with such an instrument is to tie a ribbon around one end and hang it on the wall as a decoration.

THE CONDUCTOR'S
MUSIC STAND
A word about the music desk may also be in order at this time. It should be made of wood or heavy metal so that in conducting one need not constantly feel that it is likely to be knocked over. The ordinary folding music stand made of light metal is altogether unsuitable for a conductor's use. A good substantial stand with a metal base and standard and wood top can be purchased for from three to five dollars from any dealer in musical instruments. If no money is available and the stand is constructed at home, it may be well to note that the base should be heavy, the upright about three

and a half feet high, and the top or desk about fourteen by twenty inches. This top should tilt only slightly, so that the conductor may glance from it to his performers without too much change of focus. Our reason for mentioning apparently trivial matters of this kind is to guard against any possible distraction of the conductor's mind by unimportant things. If these details are well provided for in advance, he will be able while conducting to give his entire attention to the real work in hand.

HOLDING AND WIELDING THE BATON
The baton is ordinarily held between the thumb and first, second, and third fingers, but the conductor's grasp upon it varies with the emotional quality of the music. Thus in a dainty *pianissimo* passage, it is often held very lightly between the thumb and the first two fingers, while in a *fortissimo* one it is grasped tightly in the closed fist, the tension of the muscles being symbolic of the excitement expressed in the music at that point. All muscles must be relaxed unless a contraction occurs because of the conductor's response to emotional tension in the music. The wrist should be loose and flexible, and the entire beat so full of grace that the attention of the audience is never for an instant distracted from listening to the music by the conspicuous awkwardness of the conductor's baton movements. This grace in baton-manipulation need not interfere in any way with the definiteness or precision of the beat. In fact an easy, graceful beat usually results in a firmer rhythmic response than a jerky, awkward one. For the first beat of the measure the entire arm (upper as well as lower) moves vigorously downward, but for the remaining beats the movement is mostly confined to the elbow and wrist. In the case of a divided beat (see pages 23 and 24) the movement comes almost entirely from the wrist.

POSITION OF THE BATON   The hand manipulating the baton must always be held sufficiently high so as to be easily seen by all performers, the elbow being kept well away from the body, almost level with the shoulder. The elevation of the baton, of course, depends upon the size of the group being conducted, upon the manner in which the performers are arranged, and upon whether they are sitting or standing. The conductor will accordingly vary its position according to the exigencies of the occasion, always remembering that a beat that cannot be easily seen will not be readily followed.

PRINCIPLES AND METHODS OF TIME BEATING   If one observes the work of a number of conductors, it soon becomes evident that, although at first they appear to have absolutely different methods, there are nevertheless certain fundamental underlying principles in accordance with which each beats time, and it is these general principles that we are to deal with in the remainder of this chapter. It should be noted that *principles* rather than *methods* are to be discussed, since principles are universal, while methods are individual and usually personal in their application.

DIAGRAMS OF BATON MOVEMENTS   The general direction of the baton movements now in universal use is shown in the following figures.

In actual practice however, the baton moves from point to point in a very much more complex fashion, and in order to aid the learner still further in his analysis of time beating an elaborated version of the foregoing figures is supplied. It is of course understood that such diagrams are of value only in giving a general idea of these more complex movements and that they are not to be followed minutely.

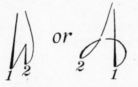

TWO-BEAT MEASURE

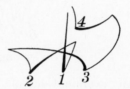

THREE-BEAT MEASURE   FOUR-BEAT MEASURE

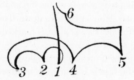

SIX-BEAT MEASURE

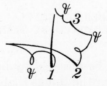

VERY SLOW   VERY SLOW
TWO-BEAT MEASURE   THREE-BEAT MEASURE

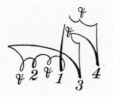

SLOW FOUR-BEAT
MEASURE

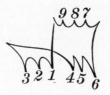

SLOW NINE-BEAT
MEASURE

SLOW TWELVE-BEAT MEASURE

An examination of these figures will show that all baton movements are based upon four general principles:

1. The strongest pulse of a measure (the first one) is always marked by a down-beat. This principle is merely a specific application of the general fact that a downward stroke is stronger than an upward one (*cf.* driving a nail).

2. The last pulse of a measure is always marked by an up-beat, since it is generally the weakest part of the measure.

3. In three- and four-beat measures, the beats are so planned that there is never any danger of the hands colliding in conducting vigorous movements that call for the use of the free hand as well as the one holding the baton.

4. In compound measures the secondary accent is marked by a beat almost as strong as that given the primary accent.

NUMBER OF BEATS DETERMINED BY TEMPO   The fact that a composition is in 4–4 measure does not necessarily mean that every measure is to be directed by being given four actual beats, and one of the things that the conductor must learn is when to give more beats and when fewer.

If the tempo is very rapid, the 4–4 measure will

probably be given only two beats, but in an *adagio* movement, as, *e.g.*, the first part of the *Messiah* overture, it may be necessary to beat eight for each measure in order to insure rhythmic continuity. There are many examples of triple measure in which the movement is so rapid as to make it impracticable to beat three in a measure, and the conductor is therefore content merely to give a down-beat at the beginning of each measure. Waltzes are commonly conducted by giving a down-beat for the first measure, an up-beat for the second, *et cetera*. A six-part measure in rapid tempo receives but two beats; while 9–8 and 12–8 are ordinarily given but three and four beats respectively.

It is not only annoying but absolutely fatiguing to see a conductor go through all manner of contortions in trying to give a separate beat to each pulse of the measure in rapid tempos; and the effect upon the performers is even worse than upon the audience, for a stronger rhythmic reaction will always be stimulated if the rhythm is felt in larger units rather than in smaller ones. But on the other hand, the tempo is sometimes so very slow that no sense of continuity can be aroused by giving only one beat for each pulse; hence, as already noted, it is often best to give *double* the number of beats indicated by the measure sign. In general, these two ideas may be summarized in the following rule: *As the tempo becomes more rapid, decrease the number of beats; but as it becomes slower, increase the number, at the same time elaborating the beat so as to express more tangibly the idea of a steady forward movement.*

By carefully studying the second series of figures given on pages 23 and 24 and by making certain that the principle of "continuous movement" explained on page 28 is observed, the student will be able to learn the more highly elaborated beats employed in slower tempos without very much difficulty. These diagrams, like the first set, are, of course, intended to be suggestive only.

SHALL WE BEAT THE NOTE VALUES OR THE PULSE?   In this same connection, the amateur may perhaps raise the question as to whether it is wise to beat the note values or the pulse in such a measure as ♩ ♫ ♩ ♩. In other words, is it well to give a down-beat on 1, two small beats toward the left for 2, while 3 and 4 are treated in the ordinary way? This question may be answered by referring to the rule given on page 25, but perhaps it will be safer to make the application more specific by advising the young conductor to adhere fairly closely to beating the pulse unless a much slower tempo makes extra beats necessary. The additional movements may be of some service in certain cases, but in general they tend to confuse rather than to clarify, this being especially true in the case of syncopated rhythms. The only exceptions to this principle are:

1. When a phrase begins with a tone that is on a fractional part of the beat; *e.g.*, if the preceding phrase ends with an eighth, thus: |♩ ♩ ♩ ♪ ♪ | ♩ ♩ |; for in this case the phrasing cannot be indicated clearly without dividing the beat.

2. When there is a *ritardando* and it becomes necessary to give a larger number of beats in order to show just how much slower the tempo is to be. The second point is of course covered by the general rule already referred to.

The conductor must train himself to change instantly from two beats in the measure to four or six; from one to three, *et cetera*, so that he may be able at any time to suit the number of beats to the character of the music at that particular point. This is particularly necessary in places where a *ritardando* makes it desirable from the standpoint of the performers to have a larger number of beats.

THE DOTTED-QUARTER AS A BEAT NOTE   Although covered in general by the preceding discussion, it may perhaps be well to state specifically that the compound measures 6-8, 9-8, and 12-8 are ordinarily taken as duple, triple, and quadruple measures,

respectively. In other words, the dotted-quarter-note
(♩.) is thought of as the beat note, some modern editors
going so far as to write $\frac{2}{\raisebox{-2pt}{♩}\cdot}$ in place of 6–8 as the measure
sign; $\frac{3}{\raisebox{-2pt}{♩}\cdot}$ in place of 9–8; and $\frac{4}{\raisebox{-2pt}{♩}\cdot}$ in place of 12–8. In
conducting these various types of measure, the general
principle given on page 25 again applies, and if the
tempo is very slow, the conductor beats 6, 9, or
12, to the measure, but if it is rapid, the flow of the
rhythm is much better indicated by 2, 3, and 4 beats
respectively.

FIVE- AND SEVEN- Although only occasionally encoun-
BEAT MEASURES tered by the amateur, five- and seven-
beat measures are now made use of
frequently enough by composers to make some explanation of their treatment appropriate. A five-beat measure (quintuple) is a compound measure comprising a
two-beat and a three-beat one. Sometimes the two-
beat group is first, and sometimes the three-beat one.
If the former, then the conductor's beat will be down–up,
down–right–up. But if it is the other way about, then
the beat will naturally be down–right–up, down–up.
"But how am I to know which comes first?" asks the
tyro. And our answer is, "Study the music, and if you
cannot find out in this way, you ought not to be conducting the composition."

Just as quintuple measure is a compound measure comprising two pulse-groups, one of three and the other of
two beats, so seven-beat measure (septuple) consists of
a four-beat group plus a three-beat one. If the four-
beat measure is first, the conductor's beat will be down–
left–right–up, down–right–up; *i.e.*, the regular movements for quadruple measure followed by those for
triple; but if the combination is three plus four, it will
be the other way about. Sometimes the composer helps
the conductor by placing a dotted bar between the two
parts of the septuple measure, thus: | ♩ ♩ ♩ ♩ ⦂ ♩ ♩ ♩ |

AN IMPORTANT
PRINCIPLE OF
TIME BEATING

The most fundamental principle of time beating, and the one concerning which the young conductor is apt to be most ignorant, is the following: *The baton must not usually come to a standstill at the points marking the beats, neither must it move in a straight line from one point to another, except in the case of the down beat; for it is the free and varying movement of the baton between any two beats that gives the singers or players their cue as to where the second of the two is to come.* We may go further and say that the preliminary movement made before the baton arrives at what might be termed the "bottom" of the beat is actually more important than the "bottom" of the beat itself. When the baton is brought down for the first beat of the measure, the muscles contract until the imaginary point which the baton is to strike has been reached, relaxing while the hand moves on to the next point (*i.e.*, the second beat), gradually contracting again as this point is reached, and relaxing immediately afterward as the hand moves on to the third beat. In the diagrams of baton movements given on preceding pages, the accumulating force of muscular contraction is shown by the gradually increasing thickness of the line, proceeding from the initial part of the stroke to its culmination; while the light curved line immediately following this culmination indicates the so-called "back-stroke," the muscular relaxation. It is easy to see that this muscular contraction is what gives the beat its definiteness, its "bottom," while the relaxation is what gives the effect of continuity or flow. It will be noticed that when the baton is brought down on an accented beat, the beginning of the back-stroke is felt by the conductor as a sort of "rebound" of the baton from the bottom of the beat, and this sensation of rebounding helps greatly in giving "point" to these accented beats.

In order to understand fully the principle that we have just been discussing, it must be recalled that rhythm is not a succession of jerks, but is basically a steady flow, a regular succession of similar impulses, the word *rhythm* itself coming from a Greek stem meaning "flow." Like all other good things, this theory of continuous movement may be carried to excess, and one occasionally sees conducting that has so much "back-stroke" that there is no definiteness of beat whatsoever; in other words there is no "bottom" to the beat, and consequently no precision in the conducting. But on the other hand, there is to be observed also a great deal of conducting in which the beats seem to be thought of as imaginary points, the conductor apparently feeling that it is his business to get from one to another of these points in as straight a line as possible, and with no relaxation of muscle whatever. Such conductors often imagine that they are being very definite and very precise indeed in their directing, and have sometimes been heard to remark that the singers or players whom they were leading seemed exceedingly stupid about following the beat, especially in the attacks. The real reason for sluggish rhythmic response and poor attacks is, however, more often to be laid at the door of a poorly executed beat by the conductor than to the stupidity of the chorus or orchestra.*

---

* It is but a step from the conclusions arrived at above to a corollary relating to conducting from the organ bench. How does it happen that most choirs directed by an organist-conductor do not attack promptly, do not follow tempo changes readily, and do not in general present examples of good ensemble performance? Is it not because the organist is using his hands and feet for other purposes, and cannot therefore indicate to his singers the "continuous flow of rhythm" above referred to? When a conductor directing with a baton wishes to indicate a *ritardando*, he does so not merely by making the beats follow one another at longer intervals, but even more by making a more elaborate and more extensive movement between the beat culminations; and the musicians have no difficulty in following the baton, because it is kept continuously in motion, the points where the muscular contractions come being easily felt by the performers, because they can thus follow the rhythm in their own muscles by instinctive imitation. But when the organist-conductor wishes a *ritardando*, he merely plays more slowly, and the singers must get their idea of the slower tempo entirely through the ear. Since rhythm is a matter of muscle rather than of ear, it will be readily understood that conducting and organ-playing will never go hand in hand to any very great extent. There is, of course, another reason for the failure of many organists who try to play and conduct simultaneously, *viz.*, that they are not able to do two things successfully at the same time, so that the chorus is often left to work out its own salvation as best it may; while, if the conducting is done by using the left hand, the organ end of the combination is not usually managed with any degree of distinction. Because of this and certain other well-known reasons, the writer believes that choral music in general, and church music in particular, would be greatly benefited by a widespread return to the mixed chorus, led by a conductor with baton in hand, and accompanied by an organist.

HOW TO SECURE A FIRM ATTACK   Coordinate with the discussion of continuous movement and back-stroke, the following principle should be noted: *A preliminary movement sufficiently ample to be easily followed by the eye must be made before actually giving the beat upon which the singers or players are to begin the tone, if the attack is to be delivered with precision and confidence.* Thus in the case of a composition beginning upon the first beat of a measure, the conductor holds the baton poised in full view of all performers, then, before actually bringing it down for the attack, he raises it slightly, this upward movement often corresponding to the back-stroke between an imaginary preceding beat and the actual beat with which the composition begins. When a composition begins upon the weak beat (*e.g.*, the fourth beat of a four-pulse measure), the preceding strong beat itself, together with the back-stroke accompanying it, is often given as the preparation for the actual initial beat. In case this is done the conductor must guard against making this preliminary strong beat so prominent as to cause the performers to mistake it for the actual signal to begin. If the first phrase begins with an eighth-note (♪ | ♩ ♫ ♩ ♩ |), give a short beat for 4 and an extra up-beat for the first note of the phrase. If it begins with a sixteenth-note, do the same thing, but make the extra up-beat with which the first tone is to be coincident shorter and quicker. If a good attack cannot be secured in any other way, beat an entire preliminary measure until the attack goes well, then adopt some such plan as has just been suggested.

THE RELEASE   The preliminary up-beat which has just been discussed is equally valuable as a preparation for the "release" or "cut-off." The movement for the release is usually a down stroke or one to right or left, or even upward. It is customary not to beat out the final measure of a composition or a complete final section of a composition, but to bring the baton down a few inches for the first beat of the measure, and then to hold it poised in this position, either counting the beats mentally, or trusting to feeling to determine the time for stopping. A slight upward movement is then made just before the tone is to be released, and it is the warning conveyed by this preliminary movement that enables the performers to release the tone at the precise instant when the baton is brought down for the cut-off. It should be noted that the release must come at the *end* of the duration value of the final note. In 4–4 a final ♩ . would therefore be held up to the *beginning* of the fourth beat, *i.e.*, until one is on the point of counting *four;* a final ○ , until the beginning of the first beat of the following measure. It is because of carelessness or ignorance on this point that composers now sometimes resort to such devices as ♩ | ♪ ꓶ ꓹ ⁻ | to show that the final tone has four full beats. In such a case, the ending ♩ | ♪ ꓶ ꓹ ⁻ | means exactly the same thing as ○ | ⁻ |, the tone being released precisely on *one* of the following measure, in either case.

THE HOLD   In the case of a hold (*fermata*), the movement for the cut-off depends upon the nature of what follows. If the tone to be prolonged forms the end of a phrase or section, the baton is brought down vigorously as at the end of a composition; but if the hold occurs at the end of a phrase in such a way as not to form a decided closing point, or if it occurs in the midst of the phrase itself, the cut-off is not nearly so pronounced, and the conductor must exercise care to move his baton in such a direction as to insure its being ready to give a clear signal for the attack of the tone following the hold. Thus, with a hold on the third beat, | ♩ ♩ ♩̂ ♩ | the cut-off would probably be toward the right and upward, this movement then serving also as a preliminary for the fourth beat to follow.

THE ATTACK
IN READING
NEW MUSIC
For working in rehearsal it is convenient to use some such exclamation as "Ready—Sing," or "Ready—Play," in order that amateur musicians may be enabled to attack the first chord promptly, even in reading new music. In this case the word "Ready" comes just before the preliminary movement; the word "Sing" or "Play" being coincident with the actual preliminary movement. In preparing for a public performance, however, the conductor should be careful not to use these words so much in rehearsing that his musicians will have difficulty in making their attacks without hearing them.

LENGTH OF
THE STROKE
The length and general character of the baton movement depend upon the emotional quality of the music being conducted. A bright, snappy *Scherzo* in rapid tempo will demand a short, vigorous beat, with almost no elaboration of back-stroke; while for a slow and stately *Choral*, a long, flowing beat with a highly-elaborated back-stroke will be appropriate. The first beat of the phrase in any kind of music is usually longer and more prominent, in order that the various divisions of the design may be clearly marked. It is in the length of the stroke that the greatest diversity in time beating will occur in the case of various individual conductors, and it is neither possible nor advisable to give specific directions to the amateur. Suffice it to say that if he understands clearly the foregoing principles of handling the baton, and if his musical feeling is genuine, there will be little difficulty at this point.

NON-MEASURED
MUSIC
The directions for beating time thus far given have, of course, referred exclusively to what is termed "measured music," *i.e.*, music in which the rhythm consists of groups of regularly spaced beats, the size and general

characteristics of the group depending upon the number and position of the accents in each measure. There exists, however, a certain amount of non-measured vocal music, and a word concerning the most common varieties (recitative and Anglican chant) will perhaps be in order before closing our discussion of beating time.

RECITATIVE   In conducting the accompaniment of a vocal solo of the recitative style, and particularly that variety referred to as *recitativo secco*, the most important baton movement is a down-beat after each bar. The conductor usually follows the soloist through the group of words found between two bars with the conventional baton movements, but this does not imply regularly spaced pulses as in the case of measured music, and the beats do not correspond in any way to those of the ordinary measure of rhythmic music. They merely enable the accompanying players to tell at approximately what point in the measure the singer is at any given time, the up-beat at the end of the group giving warning of the near approach of the next group.

THE ANGLICAN CHANT   In the case of the Anglican chant, it should be noted that there are two parts to each verse: one, a reciting portion in which there is no measured rhythm; the other, a rhythmic portion in which the pulses occur as in measured music. In the reciting portion of the chant, the rhythm is that of ordinary prose speech, punctuation marks being observed as in conventional language reading. This makes it far more difficult to keep the singers together, and in order to secure uniformity, some conductors give a slight movement of the baton for each syllable; others depend upon a down-beat at the beginning of each measure together with the lip movements made by the conductor himself and followed minutely by the chorus.

The beginning of the second part of the chant is indicated by printing its first syllable in italics, by placing an accent mark over it, or by some other similar device. This syllable is then regarded as the first accented tone of the metrical division of the chant, and, beginning with it, the conductor beats time as in ordinary measured music. If no other syllable follows the accented one before a bar occurs, it is understood that the accented syllable is to be held for two beats, *i.e.*, a measure's duration. Final *ed* is always pronounced as a separate syllable.

The most important thing for an amateur to learn about conducting the Anglican chant is that before he can successfully direct others in singing this type of choral music, he must himself practically memorize each chant. The amateur should perhaps also be warned not to have the words of the first part of the chant recited too rapidly. All too frequently there is so much hurrying that only a few of the most prominent words are distinguishable, most of the connecting words being entirely lost. A more deliberate style of chanting than that in ordinary use would be much more in keeping with the idea of dignified worship. Before asking the choir to sing a new chant, it is often well to have the members *recite* it, thus emphasizing the fact that the meaning of the text must be brought out in the singing. In inaugurating chanting in churches where this form of music has not previously formed a part of the service, it will be well to have both choir and congregation sing the melody in unison for a considerable period before attempting to chant in parts.

THE NECESSITY OF PRACTICE IN HANDLING THE BATON Now that we have laid down the principles upon the basis of which our prospective conductor is to beat time, let us warn him once more that here, as in other things, it is intelligent practice that makes perfect, and that if he is to learn to handle the baton successfully, and particularly if he is to learn to do it so well that he need never give the slightest thought to his baton while actually conducting, hours of practice in beating time will be necessary. This practising should sometimes take place before a mirror, or better still, in the presence of some critical friend, so that a graceful rather than a grotesque style of handling the baton may result; it should also be done with the metronome clicking or with some one playing the piano much of the time, in order that the habit of maintaining an absolutely steady, even tempo may evolve. The phonograph may also be utilized for this purpose, and may well become an indispensable factor in training conductors in the future, it being possible in this way to study the elements of interpretation as well as to practise beating time.

BATON TECHNIQUE NOT SUFFICIENT FOR SUCCESS IN CONDUCTING It must not be imagined that if one is fortunate enough to acquire the style of handling the baton which we have been advocating one will at once achieve success as a conductor. The factors of musical scholarship, personal magnetism, *et cetera*, mentioned in preceding pages, must still constitute the real foundation of conducting. But granting the presence of these other factors of endowment and preparation, one may often achieve a higher degree of success if one has developed also a well-defined and easily-followed beat. It is for this reason that the technique of time beating is worthy of some degree of serious investigation and of a reasonable amount of time spent in practice upon it.

CHAPTER IV

Interpretation in Conducting

INTRODUCTORY

THE CONDUCTOR AS INTERPRETER Interpretation from the standpoint of the conductor differs from interpretation in singing and playing in that the conductor must necessarily convey ideas or emotions to his audience through an intermediary, *viz.*, the orchestra or chorus. He furthermore labors under the disadvantage of having to stand with his back (certainly the least expressive part of man's physique) to the audience. The pianist, singer, and violinist, on the other hand, face their audiences; and because they themselves actually do the performing, are able to work much more directly upon the minds and emotions of their hearers. For this reason, interpretation must be studied by the conductor from a twofold basis:

1. From the standpoint of the expressive rendition of music in general.

2. From the standpoint of securing the expressive rendition of music from a group of players or singers.

We shall devote this and the three following chapters to a discussion of these two phases of interpretation.

INTERPRETATION AND EXPRESSION The word *interpret*, as ordinarily used, means "to explain,"—"to elucidate,"—"to make clear the meaning of," and this same definition of the word applies to music as well, the conductor or performer "making clear" to the audience the message given him by the composer. It should be noted at once, however, that interpretation in music is merely the process or means for securing the larger thing called *expression*, and in discussing this larger thing, the activity of two persons is always assumed; one is the composer, the other the performer. Which of these two is the more important personage has been for many decades a much mooted question among concert-goers. Considered from an intellectual standpoint, there is no doubt whatever concerning the supremacy of the composer; but when viewed in the light of actual box office experience, on an evening when Caruso or some other popular idol has been slated to appear and cannot do so because of indisposition, it would seem as if the performer were still as far above the composer as he was in the days of eighteenth-century opera in Italy.

It is the composer's function to write music of such a character that when well performed it will occasion an emotional reaction on the part of performer and listener. Granting this type of music, it is the function of the performer or conductor to so interpret the music that an appropriate emotional reaction will actually ensue. A recent writer calls the performer a *messenger* from the composer to the audience, and states* that —

As a messenger is accountable to both sender and recipient of his message, so is the interpretative artist in a position of twofold trust and, therefore, of *twofold responsibility*. The sender of his message—creative genius—is behind him; before him sits an expectant and confiding audience, the sovereign addressee. The interpretative artist has, therefore, first to enter into the *spirit* of his message; to penetrate its ultimate meaning; to read in, as well as between, the lines. And then he has to train and develop his faculties of delivery, of vital production, to such a degree as to enable him to fix his message decisively, and with no danger of being misunderstood, in the mind of his auditor.

This conception of the conductor's task demands from him two things:

1. A careful, painstaking study of the work to be performed, so as to become thoroughly familiar with its content and to discover its true emotional significance.

* Constantin von Sternberg, *Ethics and Esthetics of Piano Playing*, p. 10.

2. Such display of emotion in his conducting as will arouse a sympathetic response, first on the part of orchestra and chorus, and then in turn in the audience.

EMOTION IN
INTERPRETATION

Real interpretation, then, requires, on the part of the conductor, just as in the case of the actor, a display of emotion. Coldness and self-restraint will not suffice, for these represent merely the intellectual aspect of the art, and music is primarily a language of the emotions. This difference constitutes the dividing line between performances that merely arouse our judicial comment "That was exceedingly well done"; and those on the other hand that thrill us, carry us off our feet, sweep us altogether out of our environment so that for the moment we forget where we are, lose sight temporarily of our petty cares and grievances, and are permitted to live for a little while in an altogether different world— the world not of things and ambitions and cares, but of ecstasy. Such performances and such an attitude on the part of the listener are all too rare in these days of smug intellectualism and hypersophistication, and we venture to assert that this is at least partly due to the fact that many present-day conductors are intellectual rather than emotional in their attitude.

It is this faculty of displaying emotion, of entirely submerging himself in the work being performed, that gave the veteran choral conductor Tomlins his phenomenal hold on chorus and audience. In a performance of choral works once directed by this conductor, the listener was made to feel at one moment the joy of springtime, with roses blooming and lovers wooing, as a light, tuneful chorus in waltz movement was being performed; then in a trice, one was whisked over to the heart of Russia, and made to see, as though they were actually present, a gang of boatmen as they toiled along the bank of the Volga with the tow-rope over their shoulders, tugging away at a barge which moved slowly up from the distance, past a clump of trees, and then gradually disappeared around a bend in the river; and in yet another moment, one was thrilled through and through with religious fervor in response to the grandeur and majestic stateliness of the Mendelssohn motet *Judge Me, oh God.*

It was interpretation of this type too that gave the actor-singer Wüllner such a tremendous hold upon his audiences a few years ago, this artist achieving a veritable triumph by the tremendous sincerity and vividness of his dramatic impersonations in singing German *Lieder*, in spite of the fact that he possessed a voice of only average quality.

It was an emotional response of this character that the Greek philosophers must have been thinking of when they characterized drama as a "purge for the soul"; and surely it must still be good for human beings to forget themselves occasionally and to become merged in this fashion in the wave of emotion felt by performer and fellow-listener in response to the message of the composer.

It is emotion of this type also that the great composers have sought to arouse through their noblest compositions. Handel is said to have replied, when congratulated upon the excellence of the entertainment afforded by the *Messiah*, "I am sorry if I have only entertained them; I hoped to do them good." An English writer, in quoting this incident, adds:*

What Handel tried to do . . . by wedding fine music to an inspiring text, Beethoven succeeded in doing through instruments alone . . . for never have instruments—no matter how pleasing they were in the past—been capable of stirring the inmost feelings as they have done since the beginning of the nineteenth century.

There is danger, of course, here as everywhere, that one may go too far; and it is entirely conceivable that both soloist and conductor might go to such extremes

* C. F. A. Williams, *The Rhythm of Modern Music*, p. 13.

in their display of emotion that the music would be entirely distorted, losing what is after all its main *raison d'être, viz.*, the element of beauty. But there seems at present to be no especial danger that such an event will occur; the tendency seems rather to be toward over-emphasizing intellectualism in music, and toward turning our art into a science.* The thing that we should like to convince the prospective conductor of is that real interpretation—*i.e.*, genuinely expressive musical performance—demands an actual display of emotion on the part of the conductor if the ideal sort of reaction is to be aroused in the audience.

In order to interpret a musical work, then, the conductor himself must first study it so as to discover what the composer intended to express. Having become thoroughly permeated with the composer's message, he may then by physical suggestion arouse in his chorus or orchestra so strong a reflection of this mood that they will perform the work in the correct spirit, the audience in turn catching its essential significance, and each listener in his own way responding to the composer's message.

DEFINITION OF INTERPRETATION   Musical interpretation consists thus in impressing upon the listener the essential character of the music by emphasizing the important elements and subordinating the unimportant ones; by indicating in a clear-cut and unmistakable way the phrasing, and through skilful phrasing making evident the design of the composition as a

---

* This danger is especially insidious just now in our college and high school courses in the *appreciation of music*. Instructors in such courses are often so zealous in causing pupils to understand the *machinery* involved in the construction and rendition of music that they sometimes forget to emphasize sufficiently the product resulting from all this machinery, *viz., beauty*. The idea of these courses is most excellent, and in time those in charge of them will doubtless realize that the hearing of actual music in the class-room is more valuable to students than learning a mass of facts about it; and that if a choice were necessary between a course in which there was opportunity for hearing a great deal of music without any comment, and one on the other hand in which there was a great deal of comment without any music, the former would be infinitely preferable. But such a choice is not necessary; and the ideal course in the appreciation of music is one in which the student has opportunity for hearing a great deal of music with appropriate comments by the instructor.

whole; and in general by so manipulating one's musical forces that the hearer will not only continue to be interested in the performance, but will feel or understand the basic significance of the work being performed; will catch and remember the important things in it; will not have his attention distracted by comparatively unimportant details; and will thus have delivered to him the real spirit of the composer's message. This implies skilful accentuation of melody, subordination of accompaniment, increasing the tempo or force in some portions, decreasing them in others, *et cetera*. Clear enunciation and forceful declamation in choral music are also included, and in it all the performer or conductor must so subordinate his own personality that the attention of the listeners will be centered upon the composition and not upon the eccentricities of dress or manner of the artist.

THE BOUNDARIES OF MUSIC   It is inevitable that there should be considerable difference of opinion among composers, critics, listeners, and performers, as to just what music may or may not legitimately be expected to express. Some modern composers are apparently convinced that it ought to be possible through music to suggest pictures, tell stories, or depict moral and intellectual struggles on the part of the individual. Others contend that music exists solely because of its own inherent beauty, that it can arouse *general* emotional states only, and that if it is good music, it needs no further meaning than this. Even "pure music," the champions of this latter idea urge, may express an infinite variety of emotional tones, from joy, encouragement, excitement, tenderness, expectancy, invigoration, and tranquillity, to dread, oppression of spirit, hesitation, harshness, and despondency. A modern writer on esthetics treats this matter at length, and finally concludes:*

* Gehring, *The Basis of Musical Pleasure*, p. 89.

Is the symbolization pervasive enough to account for the steady continuing charm of lengthy compositions? . . . The symbolizations . . . mostly resemble patches; they form no system, no plot or plan accompanying a work from beginning to end; they only guarantee a fitful enjoyment—a fragment here, a gleam there, but no growing organic exaltation like that actually afforded by musical compositions.

At another point in the same work, this writer again discusses this same matter (page 120):

Music is presentative in character, not representative. Measure, to be sure, may correspond to the beating of the pulse, and the final cadence may picture the satisfaction of desires; the coda may simulate a mental summary; but the composition in its totality, with its particular melodies, harmonies, and rhythms, and with the specific union of all these elements characteristic of this composition, does not represent any definite psychical or material fact.

The majority of us would doubtless take a middle-ground position, admitting the beauty and power of music, *per se*, but acknowledging also the fact that abstract beauty together with a certain amount of suggested imagery, in combination, will usually make a stronger appeal to the majority of people than either element by itself. Many of us are entirely willing to grant, therefore, that a more complex and more vividly colored emotional state will probably result if the auditor is furnished with the title or program of the work being performed; *but we contend nevertheless that this music, regardless of its connection with imagery, must at the same time be sound music, and that no matter how vividly descriptive our tonal art may become, if it cannot stand the test of many hearings as music, entirely apart from the imagery aroused, it is not worthy to endure.* It is not the *meaning* of the music which makes us want to hear it repeated, but its inherent *beauty;* it is not usually our intellectual impression, but our emotional thrill which we recall in thinking back over a past musical experience.

Those of us who take the middle ground that we have just been presenting contend also that descriptive music can only legitimately arouse its appropriate imagery when the essential idea has been supplied beforehand in the form of a title or program, and that even then *the effect upon various individuals is, and may well be, quite different,* since each one has the music thrown, as it were, upon the screen of his own personal experience.

EXPRESSION CONCERNS BOTH COMPOSER AND PERFORMER It will be noted that in this discussion we are constantly using the word *expression* from the twofold standpoint of composer and performer, each having an indispensable part in it, and neither being able to get along without the other. But in our treatment of conducting, we shall need to come back again and again to the idea of expression from the standpoint of interpretation, and in directing a piece of music we shall now take it for granted that the composer has said something which is worthy of being heard, and that as the intermediary between composer and audience, we are attempting to interpret to the latter what the former has expressed in his composition. It should be noted in this connection that wrong interpretation is possible in music, even as in literature. One may so read a poem that the hearer, without being in any way to blame, will entirely miss the point. So also may one conduct a musical work, whether it be a child's song or a symphonic poem, in such a fashion that neither performers nor audience gain a proper conception of what it means.

INTERPRETATION IN VOCAL MUSIC In the case of vocal music, the key to the emotional content of the work may almost always be found by carefully studying the words. In preparing to conduct choral singing, master the text, therefore; read it aloud as though declaiming to an audience; and when you come to the performance, see that your vocalists sing the music in such a way that the audience will be able to catch without too great effort both the meaning of the individual words and the spirit of the text as a whole.

The great Italian tenor Caruso expressed himself forcibly upon this point during an interview for the *Christian Science Monitor*, in 1913. In reply to the question "Where do you locate the source of expression in singing?" he said:

I find it in the words always. For unless I give my hearers what is in the text, what can I give them? If I just produce tone, my singing has no meaning.

"Thereupon" (continues the interviewer), "vocalizing a series of scale passages such as are used in studio practice, Caruso commented":

Now, when I do that, I don't say anything. I may make musical sounds, but I express nothing. I may even execute the notes with a good staccato or legato (again illustrating with his voice) and still, having no words to go by, I make no effect on my listeners.

Look at the question in another way. Suppose I were to sing a line of text with a meaning in my voice that contradicted the idea of the words. Would not that be nonsense? It would be as much as though I were to say to you "This wood is hard," and were to say it with a soft voice. People have observed that I sing as though I were talking. Well, that is just what I mean to do.

"Singing, then" (the interviewer goes on), "as Caruso began to define it, is a sort of exalted speech, its purpose being to illuminate the imagery and sentiment of language. The mere music of singing he seemed for the moment to put in a subordinate place.

"By way of further emphasizing his point, he referred to a theme in Donizetti's *L'Elisir d'Amore*, which is used in two opposing situations—by the soprano in a mood of joy, and by the tenor in a mood of sorrow. He sang the measures of the soprano as though laughing. Then he sang those of the tenor as though weeping."

"But those two passages of melody cannot be identical," objected the interviewer.

"Oh, yes, they are," the tenor declared; and he quickly proved it by singing them over again with a less marked indication of the moods. "Here you plainly see where expression must start. It has to be from the words, of course. The performer puts in the feeling of gladness or sadness without regard to the notes, paying attention only to the text."

Expression in choral music is dependent upon the text to just as great an extent as in the case of solo singing; and choral conductors may well ponder upon the above words of one of the world's greatest singers, and apply the lesson to their own problems. The average audience is probably more interested in the *words* of vocal music than in anything else; and since both vocal and choral performances are usually given before "average audiences" it behooves the conductor to look into the minds of those before whom he is directing, and to adapt the performance to the attitude of the listeners.

CHAPTER V

INTERPRETATION IN CONDUCTING
(*Continued*)

TEMPO

EXPRESSION IN INSTRUMENTAL MUSIC   In the last chapter we discussed expression and interpretation from a general standpoint, closing with certain comments upon the interpretation of vocal music. But it must be admitted at once that expression in instrumental music is a vastly more intricate matter than in the case of vocal music; and in order to get at the subject in any tangible way, it will be necessary for us, first, to analyze music into its expressional elements; second, to decide which of these elements belong exclusively to the composer and which are shared by the interpreter; and third, to examine each of these latter elements in turn from the standpoint of the conductor as interpreter.

THE ELEMENTS OF EXPRESSION   There are eight elements upon which expression in instrumental music rests. These are:

1. Rhythm	3. Harmony	5. Timbre	7. Tempo
2. Melody	4. Pitch registers	6. Phrasing	8. Dynamics

Of these, the composer is able to indicate *exactly* the first four, to convey his meaning fairly well in the fifth and sixth, but to give only a relative idea of the seventh and eighth. The interpreter is thus concerned with the first four only as it becomes necessary for him to find out from the notation what the composer intended to express. On the other hand, he is considerably concerned with the fifth and sixth factors (*timbre* and *phrasing*) and has the main responsibility in the last two (*tempo* and *dynamics*). This being the case, we shall treat *tempo* and *dynamics* first of all, as being the two primary factors of expression with which the conductor is concerned.

IMPORTANCE OF TEMPO — Wagner, in his famous essay on conducting, takes the rather radical ground that everything else is dependent upon the proper selection and management of tempo. He says:[*]

The whole duty of the conductor is comprised in his ability always to indicate the right tempo. His choice of tempi will show whether he understands the piece or not . . . The true tempo induces correct force and expression.

In another place in the same work he treats the matter further, as follows: (p. 34)

Obviously the proper pace of a piece of music is determined by the particular character of the rendering it requires. The question therefore comes to this: Does the sustained, the cantilena, predominate, or the rhythmical movement? The conductor should lead accordingly.

It is doubtful whether many modern conductors would entirely agree with Wagner's statement that correct tempo always "induces correct force and expression." Nevertheless tempo is so important that probably no one will quarrel with us if we at least give it first place in the order in which the elements of expression are discussed.

In modern music the composer indicates the tempos of the various movements much more definitely than was true in earlier days, so it would seem as if not nearly so much responsibility rested upon the conductor; and yet there is still a wide difference of opinion among musicians about the matter, and in many cases the

[*] Wagner, *On Conducting*, translated by Dannreuther, p. 20.

conductor substitutes his own judgment for that of the composer, assuming that the latter either made a mistake in indicating the tempo, or else that he had not tried the composition at the tempo preferred by the conductor, and therefore did not realize how much more effective it would be that way.

FINDING THE
CORRECT TEMPO
In the main, there are five methods upon which the conductor depends for determining the correct tempo of a composition. These are:

1. The metronome indication, found at the beginning of most modern scores.

2. The tempo or mood expressions (*andante, allegro, adagio*, et cetera),which have been in universal use for two centuries or more, and which are found in practically all music, even when a metronome indication is also given.

3. In vocal music, the "swing" and the mood of the text.

4. Tradition.

5. Individual judgment of tempo as depending upon and resulting from the "quality" of the music.

Of these, the fifth, *viz.*, individual judgment is most important, and is the court of final resort in the case of the mature musician; but the amateur who has had but little experience and who is therefore without any well developed musical taste must depend largely upon his metronome, upon his knowledge of Italian tempo terms, and upon tradition. A brief discussion of these matters will accordingly be in order at this time.

THE METRONOME
AS A TEMPO
INDICATOR
The metronome* is a sort of clock with inverted pendulum, the ticks or clicks of which can be regulated as to rate of speed by means of a sliding weight. When this weight is set at the point marked 64, for example, the metronome

---

* The metronome is supposed to have been invented, or at least perfected, by a Bavarian named Maelzel, about 1815, and for many years the Maelzel metronome was the only one in existence. Hence the letters M.M., still found in many scores, in connection with tempo indications.

gives sixty-four clicks per minute; when set at 84, or 112, corresponding numbers of clicks per minute result; so that in this way the composer is able to indicate precisely the rate of speed of his composition by indicating the number of beats per minute. The indication ♩ = 84 means that the sliding weight is to be set at the point marked 84, the metronome then clicking eighty-four times per minute, each of these clicks indicating a quarter-note. But if the marking is ♩ = 64, this means that sixty-four half-notes are to be performed in a minute,—a tempo equal to one hundred and twenty-eight quarter-notes in the same composition. In compound measures such as 6–8, 9–8, *et cetera*, the tempo indication shows the number of eighth-notes per minute if the composition is in slow tempo; but in moderate and rapid tempos the direction is usually given by taking the dotted-quarter-note as the beat unit, thus: ♩. = 84. It is of course obvious that in this case the composer is thinking of each measure as having only two or three beats instead of six or nine.

THE ITALIAN TEMPO TERMS Many instrumental compositions (particularly the older ones) are not provided by the composer with definite tempo directions; and in this case the Italian tempo terms usually give at least a clue to what the composer has in mind. These terms do not of course give us the precise tempo, but by indicating the *mood* of a composition they at least help one to determine the rate of speed (*adagio*—at ease; *allegro*—cheerful; *largo*—large, broad; *andante*—going; *et cetera*). A comprehensive knowledge of these terms from the twofold standpoint of definition and derivation is indispensable to the conductor. The most common of them are therefore defined at this point. They are given in groups in order that the student may note how much the various terms overlap in meaning.

THE VERY SLOWEST TEMPO
>　*larghissimo* (superlative of *largo*)
>　*adagissimo* (superlative of *adagio*)
>　*lentissimo* (superlative of *lento*)

A VERY SLOW TEMPO
>　*largo* (from Latin *largus*, meaning broad, large)
>　*adagio* (at ease)
>　*lento* (slow)

A SLOW TEMPO
>　*larghetto* (diminutive of *largo*)
>　*adagietto* (diminutive of *adagio*)

A MODERATELY SLOW TEMPO
>　*andante* (going or walking)
>　*andantino* (diminutive of *andante* and therefore meaning literally "going less," but because of a misconception of meaning now often understood as meaning slightly faster than *andante*)

A MODERATE TEMPO
>　*moderato*

A MODERATELY RAPID TEMPO
>　*allegro* (cheerful)
>　*allegretto* (diminutive of *allegro;* a little slower than *allegro*)

A VERY RAPID TEMPO
>　*con moto* (with motion)
>　*vivo* (lively)
>　*vivace* (vivacious)
>　*presto* (quick)
>　*presto assai* (very quick)

THE MOST RAPID TEMPO POSSIBLE
>　*prestissimo* (superlative of *presto*)
>　*vivacissimo* (superlative of *vivace*)
>　*allegrissimo* (superlative of *allegro*)
>　*prestissimo possibile* (hypersuperlative of *presto*)

The expressions given above are frequently used in combination with one another, and with certain auxiliary terms, but to attempt to define these combinations in this book would be altogether impracticable. The conductor should however understand the significance of the following qualifying expressions:

> *non tanto* (not too much)
> *non troppo* (not too much)
> *ma non tanto* (but not too much)
> *ma non troppo* (but not too much)

These expressions are used by the composer as a warning to the performer not to overdo any indicated effect. Thus, *largo, ma non troppo* means that the composition is to be taken slowly, but not too slowly. *Presto (ma) non troppo*, on the other hand, indicates a rapid tempo, but not too rapid. For a fuller discussion of these matters, see the author's text books on terminology.*

The third means of finding tempo has already been discussed, (see p. 45) and the fifth needs no further explanation; but a word should perhaps be said to the amateur about the matter of tradition. The young conductor must not fail to take into consideration the fact that there has grown up, in connection with many of the classics, a well defined idea of the tempos most appropriate to their rendition, and that any pronounced departure from this traditional tempo is apt to result in unfavorable criticism. Tradition is of course apt to make us hide-bound in all sorts of ways, and yet in many respects it is a very good thing, and before our conductor attempts to direct standard works it will be well for him to hear them rendered by some of the better organizations, so that he may ascertain what the traditional tempo is. In this way he may at least avoid the accusation of ignorance which might otherwise be made. This latter point will remind the reader of the advice already so frequently given—*viz.*, "study music and listen to music a long time before you attempt very much conducting."

*Gehrkens, *Music Notation and Terminology.* Laidlaw Bros., Chicago. *Handbook of Musical Terms*, Oliver Ditson Co., Boston.

VARIATION IN TEMPO   Our treatment of tempo thus far has taken cognizance of only the generalized tempo of the movement, and we have not discussed at all the much more difficult matter of *variation* in tempo. The more evident changes of this sort are indicated by the composer through such expressions as *ritardando, accelerando,* et cetera; and it may be well to give at this point a list of the commoner of these terms together with their meanings. Obviously, such indications are of two general types dealing respectively with increasing and decreasing speed, and we shall accordingly give the definitions in two classes:

Terms Indicating a More Rapid Tempo

1. A gradual acceleration
   accelerando
   affrettando
   stringendo
   poco a poco animato

2. A definitely faster tempo at once
   più allegro
   più presto
   più animato
   più mosso
   più tosto
   più stretto
   un poco animato

Terms Indicating a Slower Tempo

1. A gradual retard
   ritardando
   rallentando
   slentando

2. A definitely slower tempo at once
   più lento
   meno mosso
   ritenuto

3. A slower tempo combined with an increase in power
   largando
   allargando } (literally, "becoming broad")

4. A slower tempo combined with a decrease in power

morendo
perdendo
perdendosi } (Usually translated, "gradually dying away")
calando
smorzando

(After any of the terms in the above list, a return to the normal tempo is indicated by such expressions as *a tempo, tempo primo,* et cetera.)

TEMPO
NUANCES But in addition to the variations in tempo more or less definitely indicated by the composer there are (particularly in modern music) innumerable tempo fluctuations of a much subtler nature; and since these are now recognized as a part of really artistic choral and orchestral interpretation, (as they have long formed an indispensable element in expressive piano performance) a brief discussion of their nature will be included before closing this chapter.

In some cases a variable tempo is asked for by the composer by means of one of the following expressions:

tempo rubato (literally, "robbed time")
ad libitum (at pleasure)
a piacere (at pleasure)
a capriccio (at the caprice)
agitato (agitated)

(The term *tempo giusto*—in exact tempo—is the opposite of the above expressions, and is used to indicate that the music is to be performed in steady tempo.)

In the majority of cases, however, the composer gives no indication whatsoever, and the whole responsibility therefore rests upon the performer or conductor. It is because of this latter fact that the amateur must study these matters indefatigably. The advent of a more elastic rhythm and tempo has undoubtedly made all musical performance infinitely more pleasurable to the listener than it formerly was; but unfortunately (especially since the advent of Chopin's music) there has been a great deal of misunderstanding as to the use and meaning of this valuable new expressional element.

Tempo rubato may be compared to speaking certain words more slowly or more rapidly in order that the essential meaning of the entire sentence may be more strongly impressed upon the listener. It must not however break up the continuity of the tempo; as one writer has said "we must bend the tempo, but not break it." Another well-known author, in treating the same point, states that*

Freedom in tempo does not mean unsteadiness. . . . We must have in music the sense of equilibrium, of stability. A careless, spasmodic hurrying and retarding leads only to flabbiness and inconsequence.

The most common kind of *rubato* is probably that in which the first part of the phrase (up to the climax) is accelerated, the climacteric tone lingered upon slightly, then the remainder of the phrase rendered *a tempo* or possibly slightly *ritardando*. But there are many phrases that demand a totally different sort of treatment; *e.g.*, a *ritardando* in the first part instead of an *accelerando*. Which is the appropriate way of delivering any particular phrase must be determined in every case by musical feeling.

The thing that the beginner is apt to forget at the period when his musical feeling though sincere is yet characterized by lack of refinement, is that these *nuances* must always be subtle, and that the listener ought not to have fluctuations in tempo thrust in his face at every turn. Indeed we may say that he should hardly know that they are present, unless he is making a definite attempt to analyze the performance. The familiar story of Chopin's breathing toward a candle flame and making it flicker slightly, with the remark, "That is my rubato," then blowing it violently out and saying "This is yours," is quite to the point in this connection.

* Dickinson, *The Education of a Music Lover*, p. 21.

It is of course understood that *rubato* is to be employed almost exclusively in moderate or slow tempos, having little or no place in rapid, strongly rhythmic music. It should also be remarked that the more severe the form of the music,—the more architectonic it is—the less variation in tempo should there be in its rendition, for in this type of music the expression is primarily intellectual. Such instrumental works (of which certain compositions of Bach and Mozart are typical) must not be played sentimentally, as a modern English writer has remarked, and yet they must be played with sentiment. The remarks of this same author may well be quoted in closing this discussion:*

Rubato is necessary in emotional music and is an excellent means of picturing longing, persuading, dreaming, *et cetera*. That is why its use is so characteristic in performing the works of the romantic school and why it must be used with su*ch* caution in the classics. The classic must be clear as daylight—the structure must be evident even on the surface; but the romantic composition needs often to be played in a veiled manner in order to produce atmosphere. In such a case the rhythm is veiled as it were, draped in gauze, but the rhythmic design is there under the veil just the same. To express calmness, decision, *et cetera*, avoid rubato.

It must now be evident to the reader that this whole matter of musical *nuance* is too subtle to be treated adequately in a book of this character, and it becomes necessary for us once more to advise the amateur to study music, both vocal and instrumental, in order that his latent musical feeling may be developed into a ripe and adequate musical taste.

TEMPO RECORDED
IN MUSCLES
In concluding the chapter let us emphasize the fact that the establishing of a tempo is a matter of muscle even more than of mind, and that before beginning to beat time the conductor should have the tempo recorded in ฝis muscular memory. Before rising to conduct a com-

* Matthay, *Musical Interpretation*, p. 88.

position, then, let him feel its tempo in the muscles of the arm and hand wielding the baton; for if not thus felt, the work will rarely be begun with a clearly defined rate of speed. This consideration receives added weight when it is recalled that if the conductor does not set the tempo, the chorus accompanist or first violinist will, and they, not having studied the music from this standpoint, will rarely succeed in hitting upon the correct rate of movement.

CHAPTER VI

INTERPRETATION IN CONDUCTING

(*Continued*)

DYNAMICS

IMPORTANCE OF DYNAMICS   Another important factor in the expressive rendition of music is *dynamics, i.e.,* the relative loudness and softness of tone. The composer is supposed to have a fairly large share in this phase of expression, and in modern music always indicates in the score at least the most important dynamic changes that he has in mind. But our observation of musical performances tends to make us feel that in this aspect, even more than in tempo changes, it is the conductor or performer who must bear the greater responsibility, and that the *amount* of dynamic contrast to be employed certainly depends entirely upon the taste of the conductor or performer.

It is safe to say that the dynamic factor is easier to control than is the tempo, and yet in spite of this fact, there is no question but that the rendition of most choral and orchestral music could be made much more interesting if it could be given with a greater variety of dynamic shading. Nor is there, in our opinion, any question but that the changes from *forte* to *piano* and *vice versa*, the gradually worked up *crescendos*, the vigorous accents on certain important tones or chords, together with those subtler shadings often referrred to as *dynamic nuances*, may become just as important and powerful a means of conveying emotional effects as tempo. Joy and triumph and exuberance are of course expressed by *forte* and *fortissimo* effects (the crowd at a football game does not *whisper* its approval when its own team has made a touch-down), but the image of a mother singing a lullaby would demand altogether different dynamic treatment.

The *crescendo* is one of the most powerful means of expression that the composer has at his disposal— especially in writing for the modern orchestra, but there seems to be a good deal of misunderstanding on the part of amateur conductors and performers about the real meaning of the term. *Crescendo* does not mean *forte;* indeed Weingartner (*op. cit.*, p. 6) quotes von Bülow as remarking that *crescendo signifies piano,*— meaning of course that a *crescendo* usually implies a soft beginning.

It should perhaps be noted at this point that there are two varieties of *crescendo;* one being produced by performing succeeding tones each more loudly than the one immediately preceding it; the other by prolonging the same tone and increasing its power gradually as it continues to sound. The first type is much commoner than the second, and is indeed the one kind of *crescendo* that is possible in piano playing; but the second variety can be secured in the case of an organ with swell box, the human voice, and in both string and wind orchestral instruments. Since some of the most beautiful musical effects may be produced by the use of this second type of crescendo, it should be employed very much more than it is in choral and orchestral music. The English conductor Coward takes the ground that the swell (a combination of *crescendo* and *diminuendo*) is the most powerful choral effect in existence.*

When the composer wishes to build up a really tremendous climax and sweep all before him by the intensity of the emotional excitement generated, he frequently

* Coward, *Choral Technique and Interpretation*, p. 112.

indicates an increase in the amount of tone, coupled with a very gradual acceleration in tempo, all proceeding by slow degrees, and perhaps accompanied by a rise from a low pitch register to higher ones. If on the other hand, he wants to let down in emotional intensity, he does the opposite of all these things. The combination of *crescendo* and *ritardando* is also tremendously effective.

In order to bring together in fairly comprehensive array the terms that are ordinarily used by the composer to indicate various expressional effects, a table of the most frequently encountered dynamic expressions is here included.

Pianississimo (ppp) ⎫
pianissimo possibile ⎭ (as softly as possible)

pianissimo (pp) (superlative of *piano*—very softly)

piano (p) (softly)

più piano (more softly)

il più pian) (most softly)

piano assai (very softly)

mezzo piano (mp) (moderately softly)

forte (f) (loudly)

fortissimo (ff) (superlative of *forte*—very loudly)

fortississimo (fff) (as loudly as possible)

più forte (more loudly)

il più forte (most loudly)

il più forte possibile (as loudly as possible)

mezzo forte (mf) (moderately loudly)

forte piano (fp) (loudly followed immediately by softly)

forzando (fz) ⎫ (These words and signs indicate that a single tone
sforzando (sf or sfz) ⎪ or chord is to be accented, the amount of stress de-
forzato (fz) ⎬ pending upon the character of the passage and of
sforzato (sf or sfz) ⎪ the composition)
> or ∧ ⎭

rinforzando (rinf) ⎫ (reinforced; a definite increase in power extending
rinforzato (rfz) ⎭ through a phrase or passage)

crescendo (cresc. or ◁═══) (gradually becoming louder)

decrescendo (decresc. or ═══▷) ⎫ (gradually becoming softer)
diminuendo (dim. or ═══▷) ⎭

crescendo poco a poco (becoming louder little by little)

crescendo subito (becoming louder immediately)

crescendo molto (becoming much louder)

crescendo al fortissimo (becoming gradually louder until the *fortissimo* point
        has been reached)

crescendo poi diminuendo ⎫ (gradually louder then gradually softer)
crescendo e diminuendo   ⎭

crescendo ed animando (gradually louder and faster)

diminuendo al pianissimo (becoming gradually softer until the *pianissimo*
        point is reached)

morendo   ⎫
perdendosi ⎪ (gradually dying away, *i.e.*, becoming slower and softer by
smorzando   ⎮ very small degrees)
calando   ⎭

con amore (with tenderness)

con bravura (with boldness)

con energia (with energy)

con espressione ⎫ (with expression)
espressivo   ⎭

con brio (with brilliancy)

con fuoco (with fire)

con passione (with passion)

con grazia (with grace)

con tenerezza (with tenderness)

dolce (gently) (literally, sweetly)

giocoso (humorously) (*cf.* jocose)

giojoso (joyfully) (*cf.* joyous)

con maesta ⎫ (majestically)
maestoso   ⎭

pastorale (in pastoral, *i.e.*, in simple and unaffected, style)

pomposo (pompously)

scherzando ⎫ (jokingly)
scherzoso ⎭

sotto voce (with subdued voice)

We shall close our discussion of the subject of dynamics with a brief presentation of a few practical matters with which every amateur conductor should be familiar.

The *pianissimo* of choruses and orchestras is seldom soft enough. The extreme limit of soft tone is very effective in both choral and orchestral music, and most conductors seem to have no adequate notion of *how soft* the tone may be made in such passages. This is especially true of chorus music in the church service; and even the gospel singer Sankey is said to have found that the softest rather than the loudest singing was spiritually the most impressive.*

Pianissimo singing or playing does not imply a slower tempo, and in working with very soft passages the conductor must be constantly on guard lest the performers begin to "drag." If the same virile and spirited response is insisted upon in such places as is demanded in ordinary passages, the effect will be greatly improved, and the singing moreover will not be nearly so likely to fall from the pitch.

The most important voice from the standpoint of melody must in some way be made to stand out above the other parts. This may be done in two ways:

1. By making the melody louder than the other parts.
2. By subduing the other parts sufficiently to make the melody prominent by contrast.

The second method is frequently the better of the two, and should more frequently be made use of in ensemble music than is now the case in amateur performance.

The conductor of the Russian Symphony Orchestra, Modeste Altschuler, remarks on this point:

A melody runs through every piece, like a road through a country hillside. The art of conducting is to clear the way for this melody, to see that no other instruments interfere with those which are at the moment enunciating the theme. It is something like steering an automobile. When the violins, for instance, have the tune, I see to it that nobody hurries it or drags it or covers it up.

In polyphonic music containing imitative passages, the part having the subject must be louder than the rest, especially at its first entrance. This is of course

---

* On the other hand, the criticism has been made in recent years that certain orchestral conductors have not sufficiently taken into consideration the size and acoustics of the auditoriums in which they were conducting, and have made their *pianissimos* so soft that nothing at all could be heard in the back of the room. In order to satisfy himself that the tone is as soft as possible, and yet that it is audible, it will be well for the conductor to station some one of good judgment in the back of the auditorium during the concert, this person later reporting to the conductor in some detail the effect of the performance.

merely a corollary of the general proposition explained under number two, above.

In vocal music the accent and crescendo marks provided by the composer are often intended merely to indicate the proper pronunciation of some part of the text. Often, too, they assist in the declamation of the text by indicating the climax of the phrase, *i.e.*, the point of greatest emphasis.

The dynamic directions provided by the composer are intended to indicate only the broader and more obvious effects, and it will be necessary for the performer to introduce many changes not indicated in the score. Professor Edward Dickinson, in referring to this matter in connection with piano playing, remarks: *

After all, it is only the broader, more general scheme of light and shade that is furnished by the composer; the finer gradations, those subtle and immeasurable modifications of dynamic value which make a composition a palpitating, coruscating thing of beauty, are wholly under the player's will.

In concluding our discussion of dynamics, let us emphasize again the fact that all expression signs are relative, never absolute, and that *piano*, *crescendo*, *sforzando*, et cetera, are not intended to convey to the performer any definite degree of power. It is because of misunderstanding with regard to this point that dynamic effects are so frequently overdone by amateurs, both conductors and performers seeming to imagine that every time the word *crescendo* occurs the performers are to bow or blow or sing at the very top of their power; and that *sforzando* means a violent accent approaching the effect of a blast of dynamite, whether occurring in the midst of a vigorous, spirited movement, or in a tender lullaby. Berlioz, in the treatise on conducting appended to his monumental work on orchestration, says:†

A conductor often demands from his players an exaggeration of the dynamic nuances, either in this way to give proof of his ardor, or because he lacks fine-

---

* Dickinson, *The Education of a Music Lover*, p. 123.
† Berlioz, *A Treatise on Modern Instrumentation and Orchestration*, p. 255.

ness of musical perception. Simple shadings then become thick blurs, accents become passionate shrieks. The effects intended by the poor composer are quite distorted and coarsened, and the attempts of the conductor to be artistic, however honest they may be, remind us of the tenderness of the ass in the fable, who knocked his master down in trying to caress him.

CHAPTER VII

INTERPRETATION IN CONDUCTING
(*Concluded*)

TIMBRE, PHRASING, *ET CETERA*

IMPORTANCE OF TIMBRE IN INTERPRETATION   Having devoted considerable space to discussing the two expressional elements for which the conductor is mainly responsible, let us now present briefly certain matters connected with the other six elements in our list (see p. 46). The two described as being partly controlled by composer and partly by the interpreter are timbre and phrasing, and we shall accordingly treat these first. Timbre or tone-quality is less important than either tempo or dynamics, and is obviously less under the control of the conductor. The vocalist may be induced to sing more loudly or the violinist to play more rapidly, but it is often impossible to get either to so modify his actual tone quality as to make his rendition more expressive. And yet, in spite of this difficulty, there are many passages in both choral and orchestral music in which the essential significance depends absolutely upon beauty or ugliness or plaintiveness or boldness of tone; and especially in choral music is it possible for the conductor to induce his chorus to bring out many more such effects than is usually done. A positively ugly and raspy vocal tone may convey a certain dramatic effect that no mere variation in dynamics is able to bring about, an example of this being found in the *Chorus of People* who sing at various points in the cantata by Dubois called *The Seven **Last***

Words of Christ. Another very short passage of the same sort is found in Stainer's *Crucifixion* in the scene at the cross. Mr. Coward has written more in detail upon this point than anyone else, and we may well quote his discussion of the topic "characterization."*

One of the distinguishing features of modern choral technique is what I term "characterization," or realism of the sentiment expressed in the music. Formerly this kind of singing was tabooed to such an extent that when in rehearsals and at concerts I induced the Sheffield Musical Union to sing with graphic power musicians of the old school voted me a mad enthusiast, extravagant, theatrical, ultra, and many other things of the same sort. These people wondered why I wanted variety of tone color—who had ever heard of such a demand from a choir?—and many of my friends even thought I was demanding too much when, in rehearsing Berlioz's *Faust*, I asked for something harder in tone than the usual fluty, mellifluous sound in order to depict the hearty laugh of the peasants in the first chorus. They were almost scandalized when I asked for a somewhat raucous, devil-may-care carousal, tone in the "Auerbach's Wine-cellar" scene, and when a fiendish, snarling utterance was called for in the "Pandemonium" scene they thought I was mad. However, the performance settled all these objections. It was seen by contrast how ridiculous it was for a choir to laugh like Lord Dundreary with a sort of throaty gurgle; how inane it was to depict wine-cellar revelry with voices suggesting the sentimental drawing-room tenor, and how insipid it was to portray fiendish glee within hell's portals with the staid decorum of a body of local preachers of irreproachable character.

Of course the battle in the rehearsal room had to be fought sternly inch by inch, but frequent trials, approval of the progress shown, and brilliant success at the concert won the day. It was so convincing that many said they could taste wine and smell brimstone.

. . . .

Contrasts of tone-color, contrasts of differently placed choirs, contrasts of sentiment—love, hate, hope, despair, joy, sorrow, brightness, gloom, pity, scorn, prayer, praise, exaltation, depression, laughter, and tears—in fact all the emotions and passions are now expected to be delineated by the voice alone. It may be said, in passing, that in fulfilling these expectations choral singing has entered on a new lease of life. Instead of the cry being raised that the choral societies are doomed, we shall find that by absorbing the elixir of *characterization* they have renewed their youth; and when the shallow pleasures of the picture theater and the empty elements of the variety show have been discovered to be unsatisfying to the normal aspirations of intellectual, moral

* Coward, *Choral Technique and Interpretation*, p. 73.

beings, the social, healthful, stimulating, intellectual, moral, and spiritual uplift of the choral society will be appreciated more than ever.

. . . .

> Tender-handed stroke a nettle,
>   And it stings you for your pains,
> Grasp it like a man of mettle,
>   And it soft as silk remains.

Before stating how to produce the laugh, the sob, the sigh, the snarl, the moan, bell effects, ejaculations and "trick-singing," all of which come under the head of *characterization*, I would say that if an ultra thing is undertaken it must be done boldly. The spirit of the old rhyme above quoted must be acted upon, or fear will paralyze the efforts put forth, and failure will be the result. In choral singing, as in other things, the masculinity of the doing, the boldness, the daring, the very audacity with which an extreme effect is produced, carries success with it. Therefore do not attempt a daring thing feebly or by halves.

TIMBRE IN INSTRUMENTAL MUSIC In instrumental music, timbre is also a highly potent influence in arousing emotional states, and we are all familiar with the fact that an oboe passage is often associated with the simplicity of outdoor rural life; that a melody for English horn has somehow become connected with mournful thoughts; the sound of trumpets, with martial ideas; and the grunting of the lower register of the bassoon, with comic effects. It is well known, also, that the skilful violinist can cause his instrument to sound an infinite variety of shades of color. But these means of expression are almost wholly under the control of the individual players and of the composer (as orchestrator), and cannot therefore be profitably discussed in a work on conducting.

PHRASING The phrase in music is very similar to the phrase in language. In both cases, it is a thought (usually incomplete and forming a part of some larger idea) which must be slightly separated from the preceding and following phrases, that it may be correctly understood; yet must be so rendered in relation to the neighboring material as to seem an integral part of the whole. In addition, it is of course necessary to emphasize the important words in a language phrase and the most significant tones in a musical one, as well as to subordinate the comparatively unimportant parts, in such a way that the real significance of the whole may be clear. Phrasing is thus readily seen to be an extremely important factor in the expressive reading of language, since one could scarcely interpret intelligibly if he did not first of all read as a group the words that belong together as a thought; and one could certainly not convey the correct idea of the group to a listener if the most important words in it were not stressed so as to stand out more vividly than the others. Although not so readily understood because of the absence of symbolism, phrasing is quite as important an element in the expressive rendition of music as it is in the case of language. In order to interpret properly the conductor must first of all determine what tones belong together in a group; must make the individuality of these groups evident by slightly separating them, but usually not to the degree of disturbing the basic rhythmic flow; and must so manage the *dynamics* and *tempo* of each phrase as to make its content clear to the listener. Many phrases are so constructed that their proper delivery involves a gradual *crescendo* up to the climax (often the highest tone) and a corresponding *diminuendo* from this point to the end of the phrase.

PHRASING IN VOCAL MUSIC — In vocal music, the matter of phrasing is comparatively simple because here the composer has, in general, adapted the melody to the phrasing of the text; and since in language we have definite ideas and concrete imagery to assist us, all that we usually need to do in studying the phrasing of vocal music is to follow carefully the phrasing of the text. But even then a warning ought perhaps to be given the young conductor regarding carelessness or ignorance on the part of singers about some of the most fundamental principles of phrasing. The most common mistakes made are:

1. Taking breath unnecessarily in the middle of a phrase.
2. Breathing between the syllables of a word.
3. Dividing a long phrase improperly.
4. Running over breathing places where a pause is really necessary in order to bring out the meaning of the text.
5. Pronouncing the unaccented syllable of a word at the end of a phrase with too much stress.
6. Failing to stress the climax sufficiently.

Mistakes of this kind are made because the singer all too frequently fails to recognize the fact that the interpretation of vocal music must be based upon the meaning of the text rather than upon purely musical considerations (*cf.* quotation from Caruso on page 44).

A comma or rest ordinarily indicates the end of a phrase in vocal music. If, however, the phrase as marked is too long to be taken in one breath, the conductor should study it carefully for some point in it where another breath may be taken without too greatly marring the continuity of the text. Sometimes in a large chorus various sections of a division may take breath at different points, thus preserving the integrity of the phrase in certain cases where this is particularly desirable. It should be noted that when a breath is taken in the middle of a phrase or between the phrases where no rest occurs, the time for breathing must always be taken from the last note of the *preceding* phrase, in order that the continuity of the rhythm may not be sacrificed.

The importance of studying phrasing from the standpoint of the effective rendition of sacred music will be realized more vividly if one takes the trouble to inquire of some of the members of the congregation how well they understood the words of the anthem or solo. The replies that will ordinarily be given to such a question will probably astonish the director of the church choir; and although he will sometimes be inclined to put the blame on the ears and minds of the congregation, there is no doubt that in very many cases the difficulty may be traced to poor enunciation and faulty phrasing on the part of the singers. The following examples are reported to be authentic instances of phrasing by church choirs:

> Jesus lives no longer now,
> Can thy terrors, Death, appall us?

The poet had quite a different thought in mind when he penned these words, with the correct punctuation marks:

> Jesus lives! no longer now
> Can thy terrors, Death, appall us!

> The wild winds hushed the angry deep,
> Sank like a little child to sleep.

What this verse means is, of course, easily seen by inserting the correct punctuation marks:

> The wild winds hushed; the angry deep
> Sank like a little child to sleep.

PHRASING IN INSTRUMENTAL MUSIC   In instrumental music we have no definite ideas and no concrete imagery to guide us; and the conductor, in company with all other students of instrumental music, will find it necessary to study his score most carefully if he is to unravel the threads that are woven together in such complex fashion in orchestral music. As implied above, phrasing in instrumental music means:

1. The grouping together of tones that belong to the same musical thought, this implying a slight break in continuity between phrases, as in language.

2. Making evident the musical significance of the group by accenting or prolonging its most important tones.

These are only general principles, however, and the details of phrasing in instrumental music cannot be treated adequately in writing because of their too great complexity. It is only through practice, reinforced by the intelligent criticism of a real musician, that skill and taste in the art of phrasing can be acquired. A few concrete suggestions are offered, and these may be of some slight help to the amateur, but they are not to be thought of as "a complete guide."

1. The first tone of the phrase is often stressed slightly in order to mark the beginning of the new idea.

2. The final tone (particularly of the short phrase) is commonly shortened in order to make clear the separation between phrases.

3. The climacteric tone of the phrase is often prolonged slightly as well as accented, in order to make its relationship to the other tones stand out clearly.

RHYTHM   Closely connected with phrasing is rhythm, and although the rhythmic factor should perhaps theoretically belong wholly to the composer, since he is able to express his rhythmic ideas in definite notation, yet in actual practice this does not prove to be the case because the amateur player or singer so often finds that "time is hard"; and there are consequently many occasions when the rhythm indicated by the composer is wholly distorted, either because the performers are weak in their rhythmic feeling or because the conductor is careless and does not see to it that the rhythmic response of his chorus or orchestra is accurate and incisive and yet elastic.

Rhythm is the oldest of the musical elements and there is no question but that the rhythmic appeal is still the strongest of all for the majority of people. Rhythm is the spark of life in music, therefore, woe to the composer who attempts to substitute ethereal harmonies for virile rhythms as a general principle of musical construction. Mere tones, even though beautiful both in themselves and through effective combination, are meaningless,

and it is only through rhythm that they become vital-
ized. In order to have interesting performances of
choral and orchestral music the conductor must see to it
that the performers play or sing all rhythmic figures
correctly, that long tones are sustained for their correct
duration, and that in general the musical performance
be permeated by that steady throb of regular pulsation
which is the foundation of all rhythmic coherence.

Modern musical rhythm is so complex in its frequent
employment of syncopations, "cross accents," *et cetera*,
that the prospective conductor must study indefatigably if
he is to unravel its apparently inextricably snarled-up
threads. We assume, however, that detailed study of
rhythm has constituted a part of the student's work in
piano, singing, *et cetera*, and shall therefore not attempt to
treat the matter further. Let us advise the would-be
conductor, however, to continue his study of rhythm
and phrasing unceasingly and never to allow himself to
be deluded into believing that an accurate knowledge of
these things is less necessary now than formerly. It
has seemed to us that some public performers of the
present day were cloaking their inability to play or
sing with rhythmic accuracy under a pretense of being
highly artistic and flexible in their rhythmic feeling.
Needless to say, the existence of such a state of affairs
is to be greatly deplored and the student is admonished
to make sure that he is able to perform every detail of
his music with metronomic accuracy before he attempts
rubato effects.

MELODY, HARMONY, The second, third, and fourth of the
AND PITCH   elements of expression as cited in our
REGISTERS   list on page 46 belong almost wholly
to the composer since he is able to indicate them precisely, and the conductor's chief concern in dealing with
melody, harmony, and pitch registers will be to make
certain that the composer's wishes are carried out to

the letter. For this reason no attempt will be made to discuss these matters further, the topic belonging to composition rather than to conducting.

PHYSICAL MEANS USED BY THE CONDUCTOR FOR INDICATING EXPRESSIONAL EFFECTS

Now that we have reviewed the elements of expression somewhat fully, what of the conductor? Shall we give him a set of specific directions for making his chorus or orchestra sing or play more loudly or more rapidly or more dramatically? Our reply is—no, not any more than we should attempt to show the student of acting or oratory exactly what gestures he is to make use of in playing upon the emotions of his audience. As implied at the outset, the thing that is necessary in both cases is that the interpreter have:

1. General scholarship.
2. An intimate acquaintance with the content and spirit of the particular work to be interpreted.

Granting the presence of these two things, the actual gestures will usually take care of themselves. The conductor Altschuler remarks on this point:

There is no artificial code of signals needed between the conductor and his men; what the conductor needs is a clear conception of the composition.

We are fully in accord with this sentiment; but for the benefit of the tyro it may be well to note again that, in general, a quickening of tempo is indicated by a shorter, more vigorous stroke of the baton, whereas a slowing down in rate of speed, especially when accompanied by a letting down of emotional intensity, involves a longer, more flowing movement, with more back stroke. Louder tone is often indicated by the clenched fist, the *fortissimo* effect at the climacteric point often involving a strong muscular contraction in the entire body; while softer tone is frequently called for by holding the left hand

out with palm down, by loosening the grip upon the
baton, and by a generally relaxed condition of the entire
body. Dynamic changes are also indicated to a certain
extent by the amplitude of the beat and by the position
of the hands. In calling for a *pianissimo* effect, the
conductor usually gives short beats with the hands close
together (if the left hand is also used), but in demanding *fortissimo* the beat is usually of much greater amplitude, and the hands, therefore, widely separated. For
the swell (⸺⸺ ⸺⸺) the hands are usually
close together at the beginning, are then gradually separated as far as possible, coming together again at the
end of the *decrescendo*.

Changes in quality are perhaps most frequently suggested by variation in the facial expression, poise of
body, *et cetera*, while phrasing is often indicated by a
movement of the left hand (thus signaling some part to
begin or stop) or by a lifting of the arms and shoulders
at the breathing point, thus simulating the action of
the lungs in taking breath, and causing the singers or
players actually to take a breath by instinctive imitation.
The manner in which the baton is grasped and manipu-
lated is of course another way of indicating these various
expressional effects, this being especially noticeable in
the case of phrasing, which is perhaps most often indicated by simply raising the baton higher at the end of
a phrase, thus preparing it for a longer sweep at the
beginning of the following phrase. But all of these
things are done in different ways by various conductors,
and no set rules can therefore be formulated.

The most important point to be noted by the beginner in conducting is that one must not direct with merely
the hand and arm, but must use the entire body from
head to toe in communicating to his chorus or orchestra
his own emotion. Facial expression, the manner of
grasping the baton, the set of the shoulders, the elevation of the chest, the position of the feet, the poise of the

head—all these must be indicative of the emotional tone of the music being rendered. But be sure you feel a genuine emotion which leads you to do these various things, and do not play to the audience by going through all kinds of contortions that are not prompted at all by the meaning of the music, but are called into existence entirely by the conductor's desire to have the audience think that he is a great interpreter. If the conductor does his work at any point in such a fashion that the audience watches him and is filled with marvel and admiration because of the interesting movements that he is making, instead of listening to the chorus or orchestra and being thrilled by the beautiful music that is being heard, then that conductor is retarding rather than advancing the progress of art appreciation; in short he is failing in his mission. One of the sincerest compliments that the writer has ever received came when he asked his wife whether he had conducted well at a certain public performance, and she replied that she guessed it was all right, but that she had been so absorbed in listening to the music that she had not thought of him at all!

The development of modern orchestral and operatic music has brought about a tremendous change in the prominence of the conductor, and there is no doubt but that his part in musical performance is now more important than that of any other type of interpreter, being probably second in importance only to that of the composer. From having been originally a mere time-beater, he has now come to be the interpreter *par excellence;* and as Weingartner remarks (*op. cit.*, p. 9) in referring to Wagner's conducting:

He is often able to transform as if by magic a more or less indefinite sound picture into a beautifully shaped, heart-moving vision, making people ask themselves in astonishment how it is that this work which they had long thought they knew should have all at once become quite another thing. And the unprejudiced mind joyfully confesses, "Thus, thus, must it be."

It will soon be discovered by the amateur that in every case where an effect such as that described by Weingartner has been brought about, it is because the conductor has studied the music and has then made gestures which were prompted by his sympathetic response to the thought of the composer. In other words, the conducting was effective because the feeling which prompted the gestures came from within, as is always the case when an orator or an actor moves us deeply. This is what is meant by interpretation in conducting; and we can scarcely do better, in concluding our discussion of the whole matter, than to quote once more from a writer to whom we have already referred.*

The great interpreters of instrumental music are those who can most nearly enter into the composer's ideals, or can even improve upon them, and who are able to give a delicacy or force of accentuation or phrasing which it is outside of the possibility of notation to express. . . . The days of cold, classical performance of great works are practically over. The executant or conductor now seeks to stir the deeper emotions of his audience, and to do so he must pay homage to the artist who conceived the work, by interpreting it with enthusiasm and warmth.

* C. F. A. Williams, *The Rhythm of Modern Music*, p. 18.

CHAPTER VIII

The Supervisor of Music as Conductor

THE FIELD OF SCHOOL MUSIC The phenomenal progress which has been made during recent years in the music departments of both the grades and the high schools of our great public educational systems, together with the fact that a large number of young men and women of real musical ability are entering the field of public school music as a life work, make it seem worth while to include a chapter upon the work of the music supervisor as conductor. The writer has long contended that the public school systems of this country offered the most significant opportunity for influencing the musical taste of a nation that has ever existed. If this be true, then it is highly important that the teachers of music in these school systems shall be men and women who are, in the first place, thoroughly trained musicians; in the second place, broadly educated along general lines; and in the third place, imbued with a knowledge concerning, and a spirit of enthusiasm for, what free education along cultural lines is able to accomplish in the lives of the common people. In connection with this latter kind of knowledge, the supervisor of music will, of course, need also to become somewhat intimately acquainted with certain basic principles and practical methods of both general pedagogy and music education.

We are not writing a treatise on music in the public schools, and shall therefore not attempt to acquaint the reader, in the space of one chapter, with even the fundamental principles of school music teaching. We shall merely call attention to certain phases of the supervisor's work that seem to come within the scope of a book on conducting.

DIFFICULTIES INVOLVED IN TEACHING LARGE GROUPS
The first point that we should like to have noted in this connection is that teaching a group of from forty to one hundred children all at the same time is a vastly different matter from giving individual instruction to a number of pupils separately. The teacher of a class needs to be much more energetic, much more magnetic, much more capable of keeping things moving and of keeping everyone interested in the work and therefore out of mischief; he needs, in short, to possess in high degree those qualities involved in leadership and organization that were cited in an earlier chapter as necessary for the conductor in general. In teaching individual pupils one need not usually think of the problem of *discipline* at all; but, in giving instruction to a class of from thirty to forty children in the public schools, one inevitably finds in the same group those with musical ability and those without it; those who are interested in the music lesson and those who are indifferent or even openly scornful; those who are full of energy and enthusiasm and those who are lazy and indifferent and will do only what they are made to do; those who have had lessons on piano or violin and have acquired considerable proficiency in performance, and those who have just come in from an outlying rural school where no music has ever been taught, and are therefore not able to read music, have no musical perception or taste whatsoever, and are frequently not even able to "carry a tune." In dealing with such heterogeneous classes, problems of discipline as well as problems of pedagogy are bound to arise, and it requires rare tact and skill in working out details of procedure, as well as a broad vision of the ultimate end to be accomplished, to bring order

out of such musical chaos. And yet precisely this result is being secured by hundreds of music teachers and supervisors all over the country; and the musical effects of a fifteen-minute daily practice period are already surprisingly evident, and will undoubtedly become more and more manifest as the years go by. The outlook for the future is wholly inspiring indeed; and no musician need fear that in taking up public school music he is entering upon a field of work which is too small for one of his caliber. The only question to be asked in such a case is whether the teacher in question is big enough and is sufficiently trained along musical, general, and pedagogical lines to handle this important task in such fashion as to insure a result commensurate with the opportunity.

THE ADVANTAGES OF AN ATTRACTIVE PERSONALITY   Charm of personality has a great deal to do with the success of many directors of children's singing. School superintendents are well aware of this fact, and of two equally capable candidates for a school position (especially one involving work with small children) the supervisor who is attractive in appearance and neat in attire, is almost sure to be chosen. We mention this fact not in order to discourage those not possessing an average amount of personal charm, but to encourage them to take physical exercise, and by other means to increase the attractiveness of their physical appearance; to enhance their charm further by tasteful dress; and most important of all, to cultivate a sprightly and cheerful attitude (but not a patronizing and gushing manner) toward children as well as adults. Attractiveness of personality may be increased further by the cultivation of refined language and a well-modulated voice in speaking, as well as by schooling oneself in the habitual use of the utmost courtesy in dealing with all people.

DIRECTING YOUNG CHILDREN   In the lower grades, it is best not to conduct formally with baton in hand, but rather to stand (or sit) before the class, and by facial expression, significant gesture, bodily pose, *et cetera*, arouse an appropriate response to the "expression" of the song. Every song tells a story of some sort and even little children can be caused to sing with surprisingly good "expression" if the teacher makes a consistent effort to arouse the correct mental and emotional attitude toward each individual song every time it is sung.

DIRECTING OLDER CHILDREN   In teaching a class of older children, it is well for the supervisor to stand at the front of the room with baton in hand, giving the conventional signals for attack and release and beating time in the usual way during at least a part of each song in order that the children may become accustomed to following a conductor's beat. It is not necessary to beat time constantly, and the teacher, after giving the signal for the attack and setting the tempo, may lower the baton, until a *fermata*, or a *ritardando*, or the final tone of the song makes its use necessary again.

A word of warning should perhaps be inserted at this point against tapping with the baton, counting aloud, beating time with the foot, *et cetera*, on the teacher's part. These various activities may occasionally be necessary, in order to prevent dragging, to change the tempo, to get a clear and incisive rhythmic response in a certain passage, *et cetera;* but their habitual employment is not only exceedingly inartistic, but is positively injurious to the rhythmic sense of the children, because it takes away from them the opportunity (or rather necessity) of each one making his own individual muscular response to the rhythm of the music. The more responsibility the teacher takes, the less the pupils will

assume, and in this way they are deprived of the practice which they need in working out the rhythm for
themselves, the result often being that a group of children get to the point where they cannot "keep time"
at all unless some one counts aloud or pounds the desk
with a ruler as an accompaniment to their singing.

THE SELECTION
OF MUSIC FOR
GRADE CHILDREN

A very large element in the success of
all public performances is the selection
of just the right type of music.   In
the case of small children, unison songs with attractive
music and childlike texts should be chosen.   When the
children are somewhat older (from eight or nine to
twelve) longer and more elaborate unison songs provided
with musicianly accompaniments may be selected, while
rounds and unaccompanied part songs are effective by
way of contrast.   In the case of upper-grade children,
part songs (sometimes even with a bass part, if there are
enough changed voices to carry it successfully) are best.
But it should be noted that the voices in these upper
grades are not usually so clear and brilliant as they have
been in the two or three preceding years, the beauty
and brilliancy of the child's voice culminating at about
the sixth grade.

THE HIGH SCHOOL
CHORUS IN PUBLIC

In planning public performances for
a high school chorus, many difficult
questions arise.   Shall the program
consist of miscellaneous selections or of a connected
work?   If the latter, shall it be of the operatic type, involving action, scenery, and costumes, or shall it be
of the cantata or oratorio type?   And if the latter, shall
heavy works like the *Messiah* and *Elijah* be given, or
shall our efforts be confined to presenting the shorter
and simpler modern works which are musically interesting and in the rendition of which the immature voices

of adolescent boys and girls are not so likely to be strained? A discussion of these matters properly belongs in a treatise on public school music, and we can only state our belief here that, in general, the *musical* development of the children will be more directly fostered by practice upon choral rather than upon operatic works; and that extreme care must be exercised by the high school chorus director in handling immature voices lest they be strained in the enthusiasm of singing music written for mature adult voices. Whether this implies the entire elimination of the *Messiah* and other similar works, is left to the discretion of each individual supervisor, it being our task merely to point out the responsibility of the high school chorus director for recognizing the difference between mature voices and immature ones.

THE PUBLIC PERFORMANCE   In giving public performances with a large group of small children, the director will need to learn that it is necessary to teach in advance the precise shading to be employed at the performance. In working with an adult chorus, the conductor expects every singer to watch him closely throughout the selection, and many slight changes of tempo and dynamics are made at the performance that have perhaps never been thought of during the rehearsal. But children are usually not able to keep their minds on the task in hand to this extent, and if there is to be a *ritardando* or a *crescendo* at a certain point, the only safe thing is to teach this change in tempo or dynamics when first taking up the song, so that the expressional element may become a habit in the same way as the tones and rhythms. This is particularly necessary in teaching the same songs to several different groups separately in preparation for a public performance in which various groups that have not practised together are to sing the same numbers.

ATTITUDE OF THE
CONDUCTOR AT
THE PERFORMANCE
The conductor must always appear cheerful and confident when conducting children (or for that matter, adults) in public, for if he seems anxious and distressed, or worse yet, if he informs the singers that he is afraid that they will not do well, his uneasiness is almost sure to be communicated to the performers and there will probably be a panic and perhaps even a breakdown. If the conductor seriously feels that the compositions to be performed have not been rehearsed sufficiently, it will be far better for him either to insist upon extra rehearsals (even at considerable inconvenience), or else upon a postponement of the performance. A good rule to follow in preparing for a public performance of any kind is this: *Go through the work over and over until it is done correctly; then go through it enough times more to fix this correct way in mind and muscle as a habit.* Too many performances are given upon an inadequate rehearsal basis, and it has happened again and again that performers have been so busy watching the notes that they have had no time to watch the conductor, and the rendition of really beautiful music has been made in a tame, groping, and consequently uninteresting manner. Our American impatience with slow processes of any sort is as often to blame here as the negligence of the conductor, the latter often arranging to have a performance at an earlier date than he really wishes to because he knows that his chorus will become impatient with the large number of repetitions that a really artistic performance requires.

THE HIGH SCHOOL
CHORUS
In directing a large high school chorus (sometimes numbering from five hundred to fifteen hundred singers), the conductor will find it necessary to study his score in advance even more than usual, for here he is dealing with large numbers of bright and lively Ameri-

can boys and girls, many of whom are not particularly interested in the chorus practice and all of whom love to indulge in mischievous pranks of various sorts. The conductor who is likely to be most successful in managing such a chorus is he who, other things being equal, has prepared his work most thoroughly and is able to conduct without looking at his music at all, and who can, therefore, keep things moving throughout the rehearsal period. We might add that if he does not keep things moving *musically*, the students in his chorus will keep them moving along other and probably less desirable lines!

SEATING THE HIGH SCHOOL CHORUS — Many other topics might be discussed in this chapter but the subject is too complex for adequate treatment except in a work dealing with this one subject alone. Let us, therefore, close the chapter by giving a plan for seating the high school chorus that has been found effective in various schools where it has been used.

Mezzo-soprano girls singing soprano		Mezzo-soprano girls singing alto	
Girl Sopranos	Tenors	Baritones and Basses	Girl Altos
Boy Sopranos			Boy Altos
	Director	Piano	

SEATING PLAN FOR A HIGH SCHOOL CHORUS

The advantages of the foregoing plan are:

1. That it places the boys in front where their less developed voices and often smaller numbers will insure better balance,* and where also the teacher can more easily see what is going on in their midst.

2. It centers all the boys in the same part of the room and thus removes the chief objection that boys with unchanged voices make to singing soprano and alto. There will probably not be a great number of these unchanged voices in any ordinary high school chorus, but there are almost certain to be a few, and these few should not be attempting to sing tenor or bass when their voice-range is still that of soprano or alto.

3. By placing the *mezzo* voices (of which variety there are usually more than of any other) between the sopranos and altos, they can be used on either the soprano or alto part, as may be necessitated by the range and dynamic demands of the composition in hand. In seating these *mezzo-soprano* girls the teacher may furthermore allow those who, although having *mezzo* voices, prefer to sing the alto part, to sit on the side next to the alto section and the others on the side next to the soprano section. If there are any boys with unchanged voices who are *mezzo* in range, they may be seated directly back of the bass section, thus keeping them in the boys' division and yet giving them an opportunity of singing with those who have the same range as themselves.

As will be noted in the plan, the conductor stands directly in front of the basses, the piano being placed on either side as may be more convenient, the pianist, of course, facing the conductor. In directing a large chorus, it is a great advantage to have two pianos, one on either side.

* The essentials of this same plan of seating are recommended to adult choruses for a like reason; *viz.*, in order to enable a smaller number of men's voices to balance a larger number of sopranos and altos by placing the men in the most prominent position, instead of seating them back of the women, as is so frequently done.

CHAPTER IX

THE COMMUNITY CHORUS CONDUCTOR

THE SIGNIFICANCE
OF COMMUNITY MUSIC
The recent rise of community music has evoked no little controversy as to whether art can be made "free as air" and its satisfactions thrown open to all, poor as well as rich; or whether it is by its very nature exclusive and aristocratic and therefore necessarily to be confined largely to the few. We are inclined to the former belief, and would therefore express the opinion that in our efforts to bring beauty into the lives of all the people, we are engaged in one of the most significant musico-sociological enterprises ever inaugurated. For this reason we shall discuss at this point ways and means of securing satisfactory results in one of the most interesting phases of community music, *viz.*, the community chorus. The development of the community chorus (and indeed to a certain extent, the whole movement to bring music and the other arts into the lives of the proletariat) is due to a combination of artistic and sociological impulses; and it undoubtedly owes its origin and success as much to the interest in the living and social problems of the middle and lower classes, which the recently developed science of sociology has aroused, as it does to purely musical impulses.

Because of the fact that community music is a sociological phenomenon as well as an artistic one, the director of a community chorus must possess a combination of artistic and personal traits not necessarily present in the case of other musicians. In particular, he must be a good mixer as well as a good musician; and if one or the other of these qualities has to be sacrificed in some degree in favor of the other, we should be inclined to insist first of all upon the right sort of personal traits in the leader of community music. In order to be really successful in working among the common people, the leader must be one of them in all sincerity of spirit, and must be genuinely in sympathy with their point of view. This fact is especially pertinent in those types of work in which one deals with large masses of men and women. The director of community singing must therefore, first of all, be a good mob leader. But if, having met the people upon their own level, he can now call upon his artistic instincts and his musical training, and by means of a purely esthetic appeal raise his crowd a degree or two higher in their appreciation of music as a fine art, eventually perhaps finding it possible to interest them in a higher type of music than is represented by the songs sung in this friendly and informal way, then he has indeed performed his task with distinction, and may well be elated over the results of his labors.

THE SOCIAL EFFECT OF COMMUNITY SINGING   One of the fundamental reasons for encouraging the use of carols at community Christmas tree celebrations, as well as other similar forms of group singing, is its beneficial effect upon the attitude of the people toward one another and toward their social group or their country. Through singing together in this informal way, each individual in the crowd is apt to be drawn closer to the others, to feel more interested in his neighbors; and in the case of "sings" where the dominating note is patriotism, to become imbued with a deeper spirit of loyalty to country. In very many cases, individuals who formerly would have nothing to do with one another have been drawn together and have become really friendly, as the result of sitting together at a community "sing." Referring to the effect of the first "Song and Light Festival" in New York City, a well-known artist remarked:*

> The movement illustrates plainly to me the coming forth of a new consciousness. Outside the park, strikes, sedition, anarchy, hatred, malice, envy; within, beauty, peace, the sense of brotherhood and harmony. . . . Community singing is teaching men to find themselves, and to do it in unity and brotherly love.

This same sort of an effect has been noted by us and by innumerable others in many other places, and various testimonies to the beneficial social effect of community singing, neighborhood bands, school orchestras, children's concerts, and similar types of musical activity have come from all parts of the country since the inception of the movement.

The impulse to bring music into the lives of all the people is not a fad, but is the result of the working out of a deep-seated and tremendously significant innate tendency—the instinct for self-expression; the same instinct which in another form is making us all feel that democracy is the only sure road to ultimate satisfaction and happiness. It behooves the musician, therefore, to study the underlying bases of the community music movement, and to use this new tool that has been thus providentially thrown into his hands for the advancement of art appreciation, rather than to stand aloof and scoff at certain imperfections and crudities which inevitably are only too evident in the present phase of the movement.

QUALITIES OF THE COMMUNITY SONG LEADER If the social benefit referred to above, —*viz.*, the growth of group feeling and of neighborly interest in one's fellows, is to result from our community singing, we must first of all have leaders who are able to make people feel cheerful and at ease. The community song

* **Kitty Cheatham,** *Musical America*, October 7, 1916.

leader must be able to raise a hearty laugh occasionally, and he must by the magnetism of his personality be able to make men and women who have not raised their voices in song for years past forget their shyness, forget to be afraid of the sound of their own voices, forget to wonder whether anyone is listening, and join heartily in the singing.

There is no one way of securing this result; in fact, the same leader often finds it necessary to use different tactics in dealing with different crowds, or for that matter, different methods with the same crowd at different times. The crux of the matter is that the leader must in some way succeed in breaking up the formality, the stiffness of the occasion; must get the crowd to loosen up in their attitude toward him, toward one another, and toward singing. This can often be accomplished by making a pointed remark or two about the song, and thus, by concentrating the attention upon the meaning of the words, make the singers forget themselves. Sometimes having various sections of the crowd sing different stanzas, or different parts of a stanza antiphonally will bring the desired result. By way of variety, also, the women may be asked to sing the verse while the entire chorus joins in the refrain; or the men and women may alternate in singing stanzas; or those in the back of the balcony may repeat the refrain as an echo; or the leader and the crowd may sing antiphonally. In these various ways, considerable rivalry may be aroused in the various sections of a large chorus, and the stiffness and unfriendliness will usually be found to disappear like magic. But if the director is cold and formal in his attitude, and if one song after another is sung in the conventional way with no comment, no anecdote, and no division into sections, the people will be more than likely to go away criticizing the leader or the accompanist or the songs or each other, and the next time the crowd will probably be smaller and the project will eventually die out. The chronic fault-finder will then say, "I told you it was only a fad and that it would not last"; but he is wrong, and the failure must be attributed to poor management rather than to any inherent weakness in the idea itself.

VARIETY OF SONG
MATERIAL MADE
POSSIBLE BY
COMMUNITY SINGING
The majority of people have no opportunity of singing except when they go to church; but many do not go to church often, and even those who go do not always sing, and only have the opportunity of singing one type of music when they do take part. Moreover, for various reasons, the singing of church congregations is not as hearty as it used to be a generation or two ago. The opportunity to spend an hour in singing patriotic hymns, sentimental songs, and occasionally a really fine composition, such as the *Pilgrims' Chorus* from *Tannhäuser*, is therefore eagerly welcomed by a great many men and women—those belonging to the upper classes as well as the proletariat. When once the barrier of formality has been broken down, such gatherings, especially when directed by a leader who is a good musician as well as a good mixer, may well become the means of interesting many thousands of men and women in the more artistic phases of music; may indeed eventually transform many a community, not only from a crowd of individuals into a homogeneous social group, but may actually change the city or village from a spot where ugliness has reigned supreme to one where the dominating note is beauty—beauty of service as well as beauty of street and garden and public building; and where drama and music, pictures and literature, are the most cherished possessions of the people. In a place which has been so transformed, the "eight hours of leisure" that have so troubled our sociologists will present no problem whatever; for the community chorus,

the neighborhood orchestra, the music and dramatic
clubs, and the splendid libraries and art galleries will
assume most of the burden of providing a worthy use of
leisure.

THE NECESSITY   Community "sings" (like everything
OF ADVERTISING   else that is to achieve success in this
                   age) must be advertised, and to the
leader usually falls the lot of acting as advertising
manager. It will be well to begin the campaign a
month or more before the first "sing" is to be held,
sending short articles to the local papers, in which is
described the success of similar enterprises in other
places. Then a week or so before the "sing," carefully
worded announcements should be read in churches,
Sunday schools, lodge meetings, and high-school assem-
blies. In connection with this general publicity, the
leader will do well also to talk personally with a large
number of men and women in various walks of life, asking these people not only to agree to be present themselves, but urging them to talk about the project to other
friends and acquaintances, inviting them to come also.
On the day of the first "sing" it may be well to circu-
late attractively printed handbills as a final reminder,
these of course giving in unmistakable language the
time and place of the meeting and perhaps stating in
bold type that admission is entirely free and that no
funds are to be solicited. These various advertising
activities will naturally necessitate the expenditure of
a small amount of money; but it is usually possible to
secure donations or at least reductions of price in the
case of printing, hall rental, *et cetera*, and the small
amount of actual cash that is needed can usually be
raised among a group of interested people without any
difficulty. It is our belief that the whole project is
more likely to succeed if the leader himself is serving
without remuneration, for he will then be easily able

to refute any charge that he is urging the project out of selfish or mercenary considerations.

PROVIDING THE WORDS OF SONGS   The leader of community singing must not make the mistake of supposing that "everybody knows *America, Swanee River*, and *Old Black Joe*," and that no words need therefore to be provided. As a matter of fact, not more than one person in twenty-five can repeat correctly even one of these songs that "everybody knows," and we may as well recognize this fact at the outset and thus prevent a probable fiasco. There are three ways of placing the songs before our crowd of people:

1. Having the words of all songs to be sung printed on sheets of paper and passing one of these out to each person in the audience.

2. Furnishing a book of songs at a cost of five or ten cents and asking each person in the audience to purchase this book before the "sing" begins, bringing it back each succeeding time.

3. Flashing the words (sometimes the music also) on a screen in front of the assembly. The disadvantage of the last named method is the fact that the auditorium has to be darkened in order that the words may stand out clearly; but in out-of-door singing the plan has very great advantages, being for this purpose perhaps the best of the three.

After the chorus has gotten well on its feet, it will probably be best to purchase copies of some larger and more elaborate book, the copies being either owned by individual members or else purchased out of treasury funds, and therefore belonging to the organization. At the first "sing" it will be a distinct advantage if no financial outlay whatever is required of the individuals composing the chorus.

THE ADVANTAGES OF PLANNING IN ADVANCE   In conclusion, let us urge the leader of community singing to decide beforehand just what songs are to be used, and to study the words of these songs carefully so as to be able to imbue the chorus with the correct spirit of each one, having at his tongue's end the story of the song and other pointed remarks about it that will enliven the occasion and keep things from stagnating. He will, of course, frequently find it necessary to modify his plan as the "sing" progresses, for one of the most necessary qualifications in the leader is flexibility and quick wit. But if he has a definite program in mind and knows his material so well that he does not need to look at his book, he will be much more likely to succeed in holding the interest of his chorus throughout the "sing."

Let him be sure that a skilful accompanist is at hand to play the piano, perhaps even going to the trouble of meeting the accompanist beforehand and going through all material to be used so as to insure a mutual understanding upon such matters as tempo, *et cetera*. In out-of-door group singing a brass quartet (consisting of two cornets and two trombones, or two cornets, a trombone, and a baritone) is more effective than a piano, but if this is to be done be sure to find players who can transpose, or else write out the parts in the proper transposed keys. When such an accompaniment is to be used, the leader should have at least one rehearsal with the quartet in order that there may be no hitches.

THE MEETING PLACE   If possible, let the "sing" be held in some hall not connected with any particular group of people, so that all may feel equally at home (there are decided objections to using either a church or a lodge room); and, in giving the invitation for the first meeting, make sure that no group of people shall have any ground whatsoever for feeling slighted, even in the smallest degree.

Granting the various factors that we have been recommending, and, most important of all, having provided the right type of leader to take charge of the "sings," the enterprise cannot but have significant results along both musical and sociological lines.

CHAPTER X

THE ORCHESTRAL CONDUCTOR

DIFFICULTIES INVOLVED IN CONDUCTING A LARGE ORCHESTRA
Conducting an orchestra from full score is a vastly more complicated matter than directing a chorus singing four-part music, and the training necessary in order to prepare one for this task is long and complicated. In addition to the points already rehearsed as necessary for the conductor in general, the leader of an orchestra must in the first place know at least superficially the method of playing the chief orchestral instruments, the advantages and disadvantages involved in using their various registers, the difficulties of certain kinds of execution, and other similar matters which are often referred to by the term *instrumentation*. In the second place, he must understand the combinations of these various instruments that are most effective, and also what registers in certain instruments blend well with others; in other words, he must be familiar with the science of *orchestration*. In the third place, he must understand the complicated subject of *transposing instruments*, and must be able to detect a player's mistakes by reading the transposed part as readily as any other. And finally, he must be able to perform that most difficult task of all, *viz.*, to read an orchestral score with at least a fair degree of ease, knowing at all times what each performer is supposed to be playing and whether he is doing the right thing or not. This implies being able to look at the score as a whole and get a fairly definite impression of the total effect; but it also involves the ability to take the score to the piano and as-

semble the various parts (including the transposed ones) so that all important tones, harmonic and melodic, are brought out. A glance at even a very simple orchestral score such as that found in Appendix B will probably at once convince the reader of the complexity of the task, and will perhaps make him hesitate to "rush in where angels fear to tread" until he has spent a number of years in preparation for the work.

DIRECTING A SMALL ORCHESTRA   The above description has reference, of course, to conducting an orchestra of approximately symphonic dimensions, and does not refer to the comparatively easy task of directing a group consisting of piano, violins, cornet, trombone, and perhaps one or two other instruments that happen to be available.* In organizing an "orchestra" of this type, the two most necessary factors are a fairly proficient reader at the piano (which, of course, not only supplies the complete harmony, but also covers a multitude of sins both of omission and of commission), and at least one skilful violinist, who must also be a good reader. Given these two indispensable elements, other parts may be added as players become available; and although the larger the number of wind instruments admitted, the greater the likelihood of out-of-tune playing, yet so great is the fascination of tonal variety that our inclination is always to secure as many kinds of instruments as possible.

The chief value to be derived from ensemble practice of this type is not, of course, in any public performances that may be given, but is to be found in the effect upon

* Let us not be misunderstood at this point. We are not sneering at the heterogeneous collections of instruments that are gathered together under the name of *orchestra* in many of the public schools throughout the country. On the contrary, we regard this rapidly increasing interest in ensemble playing as one of the most significant tendencies that has ever appeared in our American musical life, and as a result of it we expect to see the establishment of many an additional orchestra of symphonic rank, as well as the filling in of existing organizations with American-born and American-trained players. There is no reason why wind players should not be trained in this country as well as in Europe, if we will only make a consistent attempt to interest our children in the study of these instruments while they are young, and provide sufficient opportunity for ensemble practice in connection with our music departments in the public schools.

the performers themselves, and the principal reason for encouraging the organization of all sorts of instrumental groups is in order to offer an opportunity for ensemble playing to as many amateur performers as possible. For this reason, unavoidable false intonation must not be too seriously regarded.

An orchestra such as we have been describing is frequently directed by one of the performers; but it is our belief that if the group consists of ten or more players it will be far better to have the conductor stand before the players and direct them with a baton. The type of music that is available for amateur ensemble practice is unfortunately not often accompanied by a full score for the conductor's use, and he must usually content himself with studying the various parts as well as he may before the rehearsal, and then direct from a first violin part (in which the beginnings of all important parts played by other instruments are "cued in"). Directing from an incomplete score is, of course, extremely unsatisfactory from the musician's standpoint, but the necessity of doing it has this advantage, *viz.*, that many persons who have charge of small "orchestras" of this type would be utterly unable to follow a full score, and might therefore be discouraged from organizing the group at all.

SEATING THE
ORCHESTRA

Symphony orchestras are usually seated in approximately the same way, and if our small ensemble group consists of twenty players or more, it will be well for the conductor to arrange them in somewhat the same manner as a larger orchestra. In order to make this clear, the ordinary arrangement of the various parts of a symphony orchestra is here supplied. The position of the wood winds and of the lower strings as well as of the percussion instruments and harp varies somewhat, this depending upon the composition being performed, the idiosyncrasies of the conductor, the size and shape of the platform, *et cetera*.

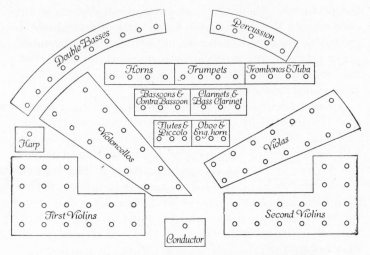

SEATING PLAN OF A SYMPHONY ORCHESTRA

In dealing with a smaller group (not of symphonic dimensions), it will be well to have the piano in the middle, the lower strings at the left, the winds at the right, and the violins in their usual position. The diagram will make this clear. It is to be noted that this seating plan is only suggestive, and that some other arrangement may frequently prove more satisfactory.

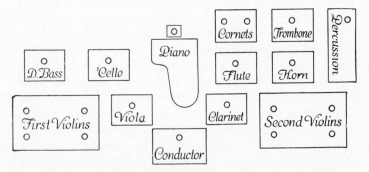

SEATING PLAN SUGGESTED FOR A SMALL ORCHESTRA

PROPORTION OF
INSTRUMENTS

In a symphony orchestra of about one hundred players, the proportion of instruments is approximately as follows:

1. STRINGS:

   18 first violins
   16 second violins
   14 violas
   12 violoncellos
   10 double basses

2. WOOD WIND:

   3 flutes
   1 piccolo } (Usually only three players)
   3 oboes
   1 English horn } (Usually only three players)
   3 clarinets
   1 bass clarinet } (Usually only three players)
   3 bassoons
   1 double bassoon } (Usually only three players)

3. BRASS WIND:

   4 horns   (Sometimes 6 or 8)
   2 or 3 trumpets   (Sometimes 2 cornets also)
   3 trombones
   1 bass tuba

4. PERCUSSION:

   1 bass drum
   1 snare drum } (One player)
   3 kettledrums   (Of different sizes—one player)
   1 triangle
   1 glockenspiel } (One player)
   1 pair cymbals
     et cetera
   1 harp   (Sometimes 2)

It will be noted that out of about one hundred players almost three-quarters are performers upon stringed instruments, and it is this very large proportion of strings that gives the orchestral tone its characteristic smoothness, its infinite possibilities of dynamic shading, its almost unbelievable agility, and, of course, its inimitable sonority. The wind instruments are useful chiefly in supplying variety of color, and also in giving the conductor the possibility of occasionally obtaining enormous power by means of which to thrill the hearer at climacteric points.

Our reason for supplying the above information is mainly in order to direct attention to the small proportion of wind (and especially of brass) instruments, and to warn the amateur conductor not to admit too large a number of cornets and trombones to his organization, lest the resulting effect be that of a band rather than that of an orchestra. If there are available a great many wind instruments and only a few strings, it will probably be better to admit only a few of the best wind instrument players to the orchestra (about two cornets and one trombone) and to organize a band in order to give the rest of the players an opportunity for practice.* It will probably be necessary for the conductor to warn his wind players to aim at a more mellow tone than they use when playing in a band, in order that the brass tone may blend with the string tone. In the case of the reed instruments, this will sometimes mean a thinner reed in orchestra work than is used in bands.

TRANSPOSING INSTRUMENTS   In dealing with any ensemble group that includes wind instruments, the conductor must master the intricacies involved in the subject of *transposing instruments*, and although this book is not the place to get such technical knowledge as was referred to in the introductory paragraph of this chapter, yet perhaps a brief explanation of the most important points will not be wholly out of place, since we are writing more especially from the standpoint of the amateur.

---

* In making plans for the organization of a group of wind instrument players into a band, it should be noted by the conductor that here the entire harmony must be supplied by the individual instruments (no piano being used) thus making it necessary to have alto, tenor, and baritone saxhorns in addition to cornets, clarinets, flutes, and trombones. The tuba is also almost indispensable, while the inclusion of two or three saxophones will greatly increase the mellowness of the effect as well as providing an additional color to make the tonal textures more interesting.

By a transposing instrument we mean one in the case of which the performer either plays from a part that is written in a different key from that of the composition, or that sounds pitches an octave higher or lower than the notes indicate. Thus, *e.g.*, in a composition written in the key of E-flat, and actually played in that key by the strings, piano, *et cetera*, the clarinet part would probably be written in the key of F, *i.e.*, it would be transposed a whole step upward; but, of course, the actual tones would be in the key of E-flat. The player, in this case, would perform upon a B-flat clarinet—*i.e.*, a clarinet sounding pitches a whole step lower than indicated by the notes. (It is called a B-flat clarinet because its fundamental gives us the pitch B-flat—this pitch being a whole-step lower than C; and it is because the pitch sounded is a whole step *lower* that the music has to be transposed a whole step *higher* in order to bring it into the correct key when played.) In the case of the clarinet in A, the pitches produced by the instrument are actually a minor third lower than the notes indicate (A is a minor third lower than C, just as B-flat is a whole-step lower). In writing music for clarinet in A, therefore, the music will need to be transposed upward a minor third in order that when played it may be in the right key; just as in the case of the clarinet in B-flat, it has to be transposed upward a whole-step.

"Clarinet or cornet in B-flat" means, therefore, an instrument that sounds pitches a whole-step lower than written; "clarinet or cornet in A" means one that sounds pitches a minor third lower than written; "horn in F" means an instrument sounding pitches a perfect fifth lower than written (because F is a perfect fifth below C); while the "clarinet in E-flat" sounds pitches a minor third higher than written. Whether the pitches sounded are higher or lower than the notes indicate will have to be learned by experience or study.

If the passage marked Fig. 1 were to be orchestrated

so as to give the highest voice to the clarinet and the lowest to the horn, the clarinet and horn parts would appear as shown in Fig. 2.

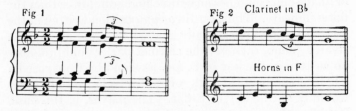

In order to make this information more specific, we add a table showing the keys of the original and transposed parts. The practical band man expresses the substance of this table tersely by saying, "subtract 3 sharps or 2 flats."

Original Key	Transposed Key	Kind of Instrument
C	D	B-flat
G	B-flat	A
D	F	A
A	C	A
E	G	A
B	D	A
F-sharp	A	A
C-sharp	E	A
F	G	B-flat
B-flat	C	B-flat
E-flat	F	B-flat
A-flat	B-flat	B-flat
D-flat	E-flat	B-flat
G-flat	A-flat or A	B-flat or A
C-flat	D-flat	B-flat

REASONS FOR TRANSPOSING INSTRUMENTS The principal reasons for the use of transposing instruments are: first, because certain sizes of instruments produce a better quality of tone than others (*e.g.*, the B-flat clarinet sounds better than the C clarinet); and second, because it is easier to play in keys having a smaller number of sharps and flats, and by transposing the parts to other keys, we can usually get rid of several sharps or flats.

In the case of performers on the clarinet, each player is necessarily provided with two instruments (an A and a B-flat—the C clarinet being almost obsolete, and the E-flat being used only in military bands); but in playing upon the brass wind instruments the same instrument may be tuned in various keys, either by means of a tuning slide or by inserting separate *shanks* or *crooks*, these latter being merely additional lengths of tubing by the insertion of which the total length of the tube constituting the instrument may be increased, thus throwing its fundamental pitch into a lower key.

In order to gain facility in dealing with transposed parts, the amateur is advised to try his hand at arranging simple music (hymn tunes, folk songs, easy piano pieces, *et cetera*) for his group of players, transposing the parts for clarinets, cornets, *et cetera*, into the appropriate keys. In this way he will also get an insight into the mysteries of instrumental combination that cannot be secured in any other way.

PITCH STANDARDS The first difficulty that the conductor of an amateur ensemble group usually encounters is that the instruments owned by his players are tuned according to various pitch standards; and he is very likely to find at his first rehearsal that his first-clarinet player has an instrument tuned in "high pitch," *i.e.*, what is commonly known as concert pitch (about one half step above standard), while his second-clarinet player has an instrument in "low pitch," *i.e.*, international, a′ having 435 vibrations per second. (There is also a third pitch which is used by many of the standard symphony orchestras—this pitch being based upon a vibration rate of 440 for a′). If the conductor attempts to have his orchestra perform under these conditions, disaster will surely overtake him, and he will not only find his ears suffering tortures, but will be more than likely to hear uncomplimentary remarks from the neighbors, and will be fortunate indeed not to be ordered on to the next block or the next town by the police force! The difficulty arises, of course, because the oboe, English horn, clarinet, and other wood-wind instruments are built in a certain fixed pitch, and since the length of the tube cannot be altered, they must either play in the pitch intended or else not at all. In the case of the clarinet and flute, the pitch can be altered a very little by pulling out one of the joints slightly (the tube is made in several sections) thus making the total length slightly greater and the pitch correspondingly lower; but when this is done the higher tones are very apt to be out of tune, and in general, if the player has an instrument tuned in high pitch, he cannot play with an ensemble group having low-pitched instruments, especially when the piano supplies the fundamental harmony. In the case of the brass instruments, a tuning slide is usually provided, and the same instrument can therefore be utilized in either low or high pitch combinations.*

TUNING   The conductor of an amateur ensemble group will find it very greatly to his advantage to be able to tune the various instruments, or at least to help the players to do it accurately. This involves not merely a mechanical knowledge of what to do to the instrument to change its pitch, but, what is much more important, a very high degree of pitch discrimination on the conductor's part. It is at this latter point that assistance is most often necessary, and the conductor who can tell his cornet player when he is just

---

* "High pitch" is employed mostly in bands; the reason for its use being that the wind instruments are much more brilliant when tuned to the higher pitch. It is encouraging to be able to state, however, that more and more instruments are being built in "philharmonic pitch" (a' 440), and the conductor who is organizing a band or orchestra is advised to see to it that all players who are purchasing new instruments insist upon having them built in this pitch.

a shade high or low, and can determine precisely when the violinist has his strings tuned to an absolutely perfect fifth, will have far less trouble with out-of-tune playing than otherwise; for a great deal of sharping and flatting (particularly in the case of wind instruments) is the result of inaccurate tuning.

BOWING   Since an orchestra contains such a large proportion of stringed instruments it will be very greatly to the interest of the conductor to take up the study of some instrument belonging to the violin family, and to learn to play it at least a little.   If this is altogether impracticable at the beginning, the next best thing for him to do is to study bowing, learning not only the bowing signs and their meaning, but familiarizing himself thoroughly with the principles underlying the art.   For this purpose some good work on bowing should be studied, but meanwhile a few words on the subject at this point will give the absolute beginner at least a small amount of indispensable information.   The signs commonly employed in music for violin, viola, violoncello, and double-bass, to indicate various manners of bowing, are as follows:

    ⊓   Down-bow: *i.e.*, from nut to point.
    V   Up-bow: *i.e.*, from point to nut.
    ⟶   Slurred: *i.e.*, all notes under the sign played in one bow.
    ⌒⋅⋅⋅⋅⋅⟶   Staccato: *i.e.*, all notes in one bow, but the tones separated.

The ordinary staccato mark (˙ or ') means a long quick stroke, either up or down as the case may be.   The absence of slurs indicates a separate stroke of the bow for each tone.   Sometimes the player is directed to use the lower half, the upper half, or the middle of the bow, such directions being given by printing the words "lower half," *et cetera*, above the passage, or by giving the initials of these words (sometimes in German).   When no bowing is indicated, a phrase beginning with a weak beat commonly has an up-bow for the first tone, while one beginning on a strong beat has a down-bow; but this principle has many exceptions. It is perhaps needless to state that correct phrasing in the case of the stringed instruments depends upon the employment of suitable bowing; and since the first violin part is most prominent and most important in orchestral music, it becomes the business of the conductor to observe most carefully the bowing of his concert-master and to confer with him about possible changes in bowing wherever necessary. It will save a great deal of confusion if players understand that the bowing is to be exactly as indicated in the score unless a change is definitely made. The first player in each group in point of position on the platform is called the "principal," and is supposed to be the most skilful performer in that section; and he is responsible, in conference with the conductor when necessary, for selecting the best bowing, *et cetera*, all others in the group watching him, and all phrasing as he does. In actual practice, this means that the players at the second desk bow like those at the first, those at the third desk follow those at the second, *et cetera*. Absolute uniformity is thus secured in each section. It should perhaps be remarked at this point that when different groups are playing the same phrase, *e.g.*, violoncellos and basses, or second violins and violas, the bowing must be uniform in the two sections, if absolute uniformity of phrasing is to result.

In addition to the bowing signs explained on page 103, the conductor should also be familiar with certain other directions commonly found in music for stringed instruments. Some of the most important of these, together with their explanations, are therefore added.

Pizzicato (pizz.) (pluck the string instead of bowing)

Col arco (or *arco*) (play with the bow again)

Con sordino, or
Avec sourdine } (affix the mute to the bridge)

Senza sordino, or
Sans sourdine } (remove the mute)

Divisi (*div.*) (divide, *i.e.*, let some of the players take one of the two tones indicated and the remainder of them the other one. This direction is of course used only in case two or more notes appear on the staff for simultaneous performance. It is customary to divide such passages by having the players seated on the side next the audience take the higher tone, while the others take the lower. If the section is to be divided into more than two parts, the conductor must designate who is to play the various tones.)

SCORE READING   Reading an orchestral score is a matter for the professional rather than for the amateur; and yet the great increase during recent years in the number of amateur orchestras probably means that more and more of these groups will continue their practice until they are able to play a more difficult class of music—this involving the necessity on the part of their conductors of learning to read an orchestral score. For this reason a few suggestions upon *score reading* are added as a final paragraph in this chapter, and an example of a score is supplied at the end of the book—Appendix B (p. 166.)

The main difficulties involved in reading a full score are: first, training the eye to read from a number of staffs simultaneously and assembling the tones (in the mind or at the keyboard) into chords; and second, transposing into the actual key of the composition those parts which have been written in other keys and including these as a part of the harmonic structure. This latter difficulty may be at least partially overcome by practice in arranging material for orchestra as recommended on page 101; but for the first part of the task, extensive practice in reading voices on several staffs is necessary. The student who is ambitious to become an orchestral conductor is therefore advised, in the first place, not to neglect his Bach during the period when he is studying the piano, but to work assiduously at the two- and three-part inventions and at the fugues. He may then purchase miniature scores of some of the string quartets by Haydn, Mozart, and Beethoven, training himself to read all four parts simultaneously, sometimes merely trying to hear mentally the successive harmonies as he looks at the score, but most often playing the parts on the piano. After mastering four voices in this way, he is ready to begin on one of the slow movements of a Haydn symphony.

In examining an orchestral score, it will be noted at once that the string parts are always together at the bottom of the page, while the wood-wind material is at the top. Since the strings furnish the most important parts of the harmonic structure for so much of the time, our amateur will at first play only the string parts, with the possible addition of the flute, oboe, and certain other non-transposed voices a little later on. But as he gains facility he will gradually be able to take in all the parts and to include at least a sort of summary of them all in his playing. The student is advised to purchase a number of the Haydn and Mozart symphonies either in the form of pocket editions or in the regular conductor's score, and to practise on these until he feels quite sure of himself. By this time he will be ready to try his hand at a modern score, which will be found not only to contain parts for more instruments, but many more divided parts for the strings. Meanwhile, he is, of course, taking every possible opportunity of attending concerts given by symphony orchestras, and is begging, borrowing, or buying the scores of as many of the compositions as possible, studying them in advance, and taking keen delight in following them at the performance; perhaps even imagining himself to be the conductor, and having visions of changes in interpretation that he would like to make if he were directing. As the result of several years of this sort of study, even an amateur may get to the point where he is able to conduct an orchestra from a full score with some degree of skill, and hence with some little satisfaction both to himself and to the performers.

TABLE SHOWING RANGES OF ORCHESTRAL INSTRUMENTS

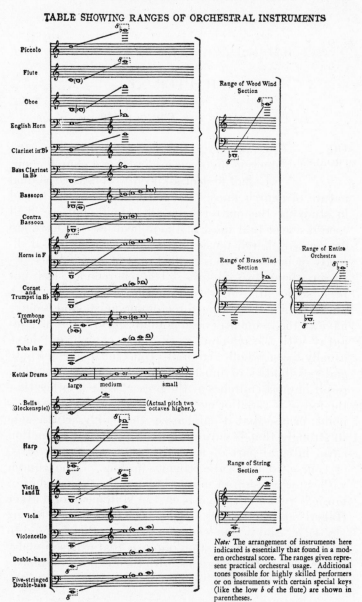

Note: The arrangement of instruments here indicated is essentially that found in a modern orchestral score. The ranges given represent practical orchestral usage. Additional tones possible for highly skilled performers or on instruments with certain special keys (like the low *b* of the flute) are shown in parentheses.

CHAPTER XI

Directing the Church Choir

THE PROBLEM In taking up the special problems of conducting involved in directing a church choir, we shall first of all need to consider the dual nature of church music—its religio-artistic aspect, and in studying the matter from this standpoint we shall soon discover that most of the difficulties that have encompassed church music in the past can be traced directly or indirectly to a conflict or a lack of balance between these two factors. The churchman has not been sufficiently interested in the *art* side of church music, while the music director, organist, and singers have all too frequently been not only entirely out of sympathy with the religious work of the church, but have usually been wholly ignorant concerning the purpose and possibilities of music in the church service. The result in most churches at the present time is either that the music is vapid or even offensive from the art standpoint; or else that it emphasizes the purely artistic side so strongly that it entirely fails to perform its function as an integral part of a service whose *raison d'être* is, of course, to inculcate religious feeling. "The church wishes for worship in music, but not for the worship of music," is said to have been the statement of Father Haberl at the Saint Cecilia Conference in Mainz (1884).* And it is indeed a far cry from this demand to the very evident deification of music that exists in many of our modern city churches, with their expensive soloists and their utter failure to cause music to minister as "the

* Quoted by Curwen on the title page of *Studies in Worship Music* (second series).

handmaid of religion." The problem is not a new one, and in a book written about a century ago the author says:*

The guiding rule which ought always to be present to the mind of a clergyman should also be held in mind by all good musicians who would help the church's object, and not employ the sacred building merely as a place where all kind of sounds that tickle the ear can be heard. All kinds of music are suitable for sacred use that do not raise secular associations. A *Largo*, an *Adagio*, a *Grave*, an *Andante*, an *Allegro*, a fugal or a non-fugal composition can all be performed in the Church but should one and all be of a staid and dignified character throughout, elevated and sober, and of such a nature that any preacher of note could say: "This splendid music is a fitting introduction to my discourse"; or "After such singing my lips had better be closed, and the spirit left to its own silent worship."

A distinguished modern writer voices the same thought in the following words:*

The singing of the choir must be contrived and felt as part of the office of prayer. The spirit and direction of the whole service for the day must be unified; the music must be a vital and organic element in this unit.

But in most churches music does not function in this ideal way and in many cases (especially in non-liturgical churches) there is no unity whatever in the service, and the music is evidently both performed and listened to from a purely art standpoint; or else it is so crude and inartistic as to be actually painful to the worshiper with refined sensibilities.

THE REMEDY   What is to be the remedy for this state of affairs? Or is there no remedy, and must we go on, either enduring tortures artistically, or suffering spiritually? We are not omniscient, but we venture to assert that conditions might be caused to improve by the adoption of several changes of procedure that are herewith recommended.

1. Educate the minister musically during his general and professional training, causing him not only to acquire a certain amount of technical musical ability, but attempting also to cultivate in him that intangible something

* Thibaut, *Purity in Music*, translated by Broadhouse, p. 24.
* Dickinson, *Music in the History of the Western Church*, p. 401.

which we call musical taste. A few seminaries—notably the Hartford Theological Seminary, the Boston University Department of Religious Education and the Western Theological Seminary at Pittsburgh—are doing pioneer work along this line, but they are the exception rather than the rule, and the thing must be done by all if the desired result is to obtain in the future.

2. Encourage the organization of chorus choirs composed largely of those who belong to or attend the church and are therefore vitally interested in its work.

3. Select more churchly music, *i.e.*, a type of music which when appropriately rendered will tend to bring about a mood of worship. This will often mean a simpler style of music; it may mean more *a cappella* singing; and it undoubtedly implies music that is fundamentally *sincere*. That many of our modern sacred solos and anthems fail in this latter respect must be evident to any one who has given the matter any thought whatever.

4. Let the church make an attempt to secure as its musical director one who possesses a type of seriousness and high-mindedness that will make him sympathetic with what the church is trying to do, thus enabling him to minister to the people through music even as the priest or preacher does through words of consolation or inspiration. We admit that this sort of a man (who is at the same time unimpeachable in his musical authority) is often hard to find; but that the two elements are incompatible, and that such a type of choir director cannot be trained, we absolutely refuse to believe. If the church sufficiently recognizes the failure of music as now frequently administered, and makes a strong enough demand for leaders of a different type, they are bound to be forthcoming.

CORRELATING THE MUSIC WITH THE REST OF THE SERVICE Having trained our minister from a musical standpoint, organized a chorus choir, selected appropriate music, and secured the right type of choir leader, let us now make a strenuous attempt to correlate the musical with the non-musical parts of the service; and if we succeed in our effort at this point also, our task will be at least in sight of completion. This desirable correlation will only result if both minister and musician are willing to work together amicably, each recognizing the rights of the other, and both willing to give in upon occasion in order to make the service as a whole work out more smoothly. Many humorous stories are told, the point of which is based upon the absolute incongruity of the various parts of the church service. The writer remembers most vividly an incident that occurred during the first year of the Great War, in the church in which he was at that time the choirmaster. The choir had just finished singing an anthem written by an English composer as a prayer for peace,* the concluding strains being sung to the words "Give peace, O God, give peace again! Amen." As the choir sat down, after an effective rendition of the anthem, there was a hush in the congregation, showing that the message of the music had gone home to the hearers. But a moment later the spell was rudely broken, as the minister rose, and in a stentorian voice proclaimed the text of the day—"For I come not to bring peace into the world, but a sword."

The responsibility in this case rested as much upon the shoulders of the choir director as upon those of the preacher, for he should at least have taken the trouble to acquaint his coworker with the nature of the anthem, so that some reference might have been made to the subject in either the prayer or scripture reading or in some of the hymns, if not in the sermon itself. It is perhaps not always feasible to have sermon and anthem agree absolutely in subject, but it is entirely possible to avoid such occurrences as that cited above, if even a small amount of thought is given to the matter of correlation each week. Surely the choir leader could at least provide the minister with the titles of the anthems and solos to be rendered.

DIFFICULTIES INVOLVED IN THE CHORUS CHOIR   In advocating a return to the volunteer chorus choir instead of the salaried solo quartet, we are well aware of the disadvantages that are likely to accompany any attempt along this line. We know that the chorus choir composed of volunteers is often poorly balanced, usually contains for the most part indifferent voices and often unskilful readers, and frequently consists largely of

* John E. West, *O God of Love, O King of Peace.*

giddy young girls, whose main object in singing in the choir is obviously not based upon their interest in the spiritual advancement of the community! But we believe that under the right type of leadership most of these bad conditions will in time disappear, and that, through the chorus choir, music may well become a vitalizing force in the life of many a church in which a revitalizing process is badly needed.

In order to make ourselves perfectly clear, let us summarize at this point the qualifications especially needed by the conductor of a volunteer church chorus.

1.   He must be a reasonably good musician, possessing not only familiarity with music in general, but in particular an intimate knowledge of vocal music, and knowing at least the fundamentals of voice training.

2.   He must understand the purpose of church music, and must be in sympathy with the religious work of the church.

3.   He must be young in spirit, and thus be able to take a sympathetic attitude toward the members of his choir as human beings, and particularly as human beings who are still young, inexperienced, and frequently thoughtless.   This implies, of course, a certain amount of personal magnetism and this is as necessary in the volunteer choir for holding the membership together and securing regular attendance as it is for inspiring them musically.

THE DANGER OF   One of the chief difficulties encountered
INDIVIDUALISM   in more or less all choral organizations, and especially in the volunteer church choir, is the tendency on the part of many members to do all they possibly can in the way of dress, actions, loud singing, and lack of voice blending, to call attention to themselves as individuals.   This not only results in frequent offense to the eye of the worshiper because of clashing color combinations (the remedy for which is, of course, some uniform method of dressing or perhaps a vestment), but what is even more serious, it often causes a lack of voice blending that seriously interferes with both the religious and the artistic effect of the music.   For this latter state of affairs there is no remedy except to learn to listen to individual voices, and when some voice

does not blend with the rest, to let the person who owns it know that he must either sing very softly or else stop entirely. This can often be accomplished by a look in the direction of the singer who is causing the trouble; but if this does not suffice, then a private admonition may be necessary—and here we have a situation in which the diplomacy and the good humor of the conductor must be exercised to the utmost, especially if the offending voice belongs to a prominent member of, and perhaps a liberal contributor to, the church. In such a case, one may sometimes, without unduly compromising one's reputation for veracity, inform the offending member that his method of singing is very bad indeed for his voice, and if persisted in will surely ruin that organ!

Needless to say, the conductor must exercise the utmost tactfulness in dealing with such matters as these, but it is our belief that if he insists strongly enough in the rehearsal upon a unified body of tone from each part, and backs this up by private conversations with individual members, with perhaps a free lesson or two in correct voice placement, or even the elimination of one or two utterly hopeless voices, a fine quality of voice blending will eventually result. It might be remarked at this point that such desirable homogeneity of tone will only eventuate if each individual member of the choir becomes willing to submerge his own voice in the total effect of his part; and that learning to give way in this fashion for the sake of the larger good of the entire group is one of the most valuable social lessons to be learned by the young men and women of today. It is the business of the choir leader to drive home this lesson whenever necessary. It is also his task to see to it that no member of his choir by his actions causes any interference with the worship of the congregation. In plain speech, it is his duty to see to it that choir members conduct themselves in a manner appropriate to their position, and that they do not by whispering, laughing, note writing, and other

similar frivolities, hinder in any way the development of a spirit of reverent devotion on the part of the
congregation.

SOLO SINGING   Another type of undesirable individu-
IN THE CHURCH   alism is to be found in the case of the
SERVICE   church solo singer. We have no quarrel with the sacred solo when sung in such a way as to
move the hearts of the congregation to a more sincere
attitude of devotion; and we are entirely willing to
grant that the sacred solo has the inherent possibility of
becoming as pregnant with religious fervor as the sermon
itself, and may indeed, because of its esthetic and emotional appeal, convey a message of comfort or of inspiration to many a heart that might remain untouched by
the appeal of a merely intellectual sermon. But it has
been our observation that the usual church solo very seldom functions in this way; that the singer usually con-
siders it only as an opportunity to show how well he can
perform; that he seldom thinks very much about the
words; that the selections are usually not chosen because they are appropriate to the remainder of the service but because they are "effective" or perhaps because
they are well adapted to the voice or the style of the
singer; and that our congregations have grown so accustomed to this sort of thing that the performance of a
sacred solo is now usually listened to, commented upon,
and criticized in exactly the same way in the church
service as would be the case at a concert performance.

Instead of thinking, "I am delivering a *message*,"
the singer is only too palpably saying to us, "*I* am singing a *solo*, don't you think I am doing it well?"

The remedy for this condition of affairs is the same as
that which we have been recommending for church
music in general, and before church solo singing can be
commended in very glowing terms as a method of assist-

ing the congregation to become more thoughtful, more fervent in their devotional attitude, we must have:

1. More appropriate selections.
2. A more sincerely reverent and a more thoroughly non-egoistic attitude on the part of the soloists.

Because these things are so difficult of attainment under present conditions our feeling is that, all in all, chorus music is probably considerably more effective as a vehicle for making a religio-esthetic appeal, than solo singing.

PROGRESS IN PUBLIC SCHOOL MUSIC AS RELATED TO CHURCH CHOIRS The public schools are doing very much more in the way of teaching music than formerly, and in many places consistent work is being carried on as the result of which the children now in school are learning to read music notation somewhat fluently, to use their voices correctly, and are cultivating as well a certain amount of taste in music. Because of this musical activity in the public schools, our task of organizing and directing volunteer church choirs should be very much simplified in the near future. Community singing will help at this point also, and the very much larger number of boys and girls who are receiving training as the result of the development of high school music, ought to make it considerably easier to secure the right type of choir director in the future than has been the case in the past. As a result of the present widespread interest in music and music study, it should be possible also to get very much better congregational singing, and withal to interest the congregation (and the preacher!) in a better type of music. All in all, the outlook is extremely promising and we venture to predict a great improvement in all that pertains to church music during the next quarter century.

IMPORTANCE OF CONGREGATIONAL SINGING   Let us close this discussion by urging the choir director to remember that the most important music, at least in the Protestant church, is the congregational singing; and to consider the fact that if music is to help people worship without becoming a substitute for worship, it will be necessary for him not only to inspire his choir with high ideals of church music, but also to devise means of inducing the congregation to take part in the singing to a much greater extent than is now the case in most churches.   It is usually true that the finer the choir, and the more elaborate the accompaniment, the less hearty is the congregational singing.   If there is to be steady growth in the efficiency of chorus choirs, therefore, it will not be surprising if congregational singing sometimes falls off in volume and enthusiasm. The reasons for such a decline are: First, because the people take no responsibility for the singing, knowing that it will go well whether they join in or not; second, because the choir often sings so well that the people would rather listen than take part; third, because the director frequently stands with his back to the congregation and apparently does not expect much singing from them; and fourth, because the choir leader often insists upon a highly musical interpretation of the hymns, this involving the carrying over of phrases, *et cetera.*   These latter things may well be done after a long period of training, but in the early stages the way to arouse interest in congregational singing is not to insist too strongly upon the purely artistic aspects, but to remember that most of the congregation are musically untrained and not only do not see the point to all these refinements, but will frequently become discouraged and stop singing entirely if too many of them are insisted upon.   It will be well also to apply to this type of group singing the principles already discussed in connection with community "sings," having the congregation sing alone part of the time, having a stanza sung as a solo occasionally, making use of antiphonal effects, and in other ways introducing variety and placing more responsibility upon the congregation; and, most important of all, calling attention more frequently to the words of the hymns, either the preacher or the choir leader sometimes giving the stories of their origin, and in other ways attempting to interest the congregation in the meaning of the hymn as a poem. Perhaps a more careful selection of the hymns would help also, especially if a consistent attempt were to be made to give the congregation an opportunity of practising the more musical tunes, so that they would come to feel familiar with them and at ease in singing them. If the choir director will take the trouble to go through the hymn book and select forty or fifty really fine hymns and tunes that are not being used, suggesting to the minister that these be sung sometimes in connection with the more familiar ones, he will very often find the minister more than willing to meet him half way in the matter. In these various ways the choir leader and the minister may by consistent coöperation inspire the congregation to the point where the vocal response is as hearty and as *heartfelt* as it used to be in the olden days.

CHAPTER XII

THE BOY CHOIR AND ITS PROBLEMS

THE PROBLEMS The two special problems connected with directing a boy choir are:

1. Becoming intimately acquainted with the compass, registers, possibilities, and limitations of the boy's voice.

2. Finding out how to manage the boys themselves so as to keep them good-natured, well-behaved, interested, and hard at work.

To these two might be added a third—namely, the problem of becoming familiar with the liturgy of the particular church in which the choir sings, since male choirs are to be found most often in liturgical churches. But since this will vary widely in the case of different sects, we shall not concern ourselves with it, but will be content with giving a brief discussion of each of the other points.

PECULIARITIES OF The child voice is not merely a
THE CHILD VOICE miniature adult voice, but is an instrument of quite different character. In the first place, it is not nearly so individualistic in timbre as the adult voice, and because of the far greater homogeneity of voice quality that obtains in children's singing, it is much easier to secure blending of tone, the effect being that of one voice rather than of a number of voices in combination. This is a disadvantage from the standpoint of variety of color in producing certain emotional effects, but it is in some ways an advantage in the church service, especially in churches where the ideal is to make the entire procedure as impersonal and formal as possible. In the second place, the child voice is good only in the upper register—the chest

tones being throaty, unpleasant, and frequently off pitch. In the third place, the child voice is immature, and his vocal organs are much more likely to be injured by overstraining. When directed by a competent voice trainer, however, the effect of a large group of children singing together is most striking, and their pure, fresh, flutelike tones, combined with the appearance of purity and innocence which they present to the eye, bring many a thrill to the heart and not infrequently a tear to the eye of the worshiper.

THE BOY VOICE IN THE CHURCH CHOIR   In many European churches, and in a considerable number in the United States, it is customary to have boys with unchanged voices sing the soprano part, men with trained falsetto voices (called male altos) taking the alto,* while the tenor and bass parts are, of course, sung by men as always. Since the child voice is only useful when the tones are produced with relaxed muscles, and since the resonance cavities have not developed sufficiently to give the voice a great deal of power, it is possible for a few men on each of the lower parts to sing with from twenty to thirty boys on the soprano part. Six basses, four tenors, and four altos will easily balance twenty-five boy sopranos, if all voices are of average power.

THE NECESSITY OF BEING A VOICE TRAINER   There is one difference between the mixed choir of adult voices and the boy choir that should be noted at the outset by the amateur. It is that, in the former, the

---

* In many male choirs the alto part is sung by boys; but this does not result in a fine blending of parts, because of the fact, as already noted in the above paragraph, that the boy's voice is good only in its upper register. It may be of interest to the reader to know that in places where there are no adult male altos, these voices may be trained with comparative ease. All that is needed is a baritone or bass who has no particular ambitions in the direction of solo singing (the extensive use of the falsetto voice is detrimental to the lower tones); who is a good reader; and who is willing to vocalize in his falsetto voice a half hour a day for a few months. The chief obstacle that is likely to be encountered in training male altos is the fact that the men are apt to regard falsetto singing as effeminate.

choir leader is working with mature men and women, most of whom have probably learned to use their voices as well as they ever will; but in directing a boy choir, the sopranos must be taught not only the actual music to be sung at the church service, but, what is much more difficult, they must be trained in the essentials of correct breathing, tone placement, *et cetera*, from the ground up. Hence the absolute necessity of the choirmaster being a voice specialist. He need not have a fine solo voice, but he must know the essentials of good singing, and must be able to demonstrate with his own voice what he means by purity of vowel, clearness of enunciation, *et cetera*. These things are probably always best taught by imitation, even in the case of adults; but when dealing with a crowd of lively American boys, imitation is practically the only method that *can* be used successfully. We shall not attempt to give information regarding this highly important matter in the present volume, because it is far too complex and difficult to be taken up in anything short of a treatise and because, moreover, the art of singing cannot be taught in a book. The student who is ambitious to become the director of a boy choir is advised, first, to study singing for a period of years, and second, to read several good books upon the training of children's voices. There are a number of books of this character, some of the best ones being included in the reference list in Appendix A (p. 164).

THE DIFFERENCE
BETWEEN THE VOICES
OF BOYS AND GIRLS
The child's larynx grows steadily up to the age of about six, but at this time growth ceases, and until puberty the vocal cords, larynx, and throat muscles develop in strength and flexibility, without increasing appreciably in size. This means that from six until the beginning of adolescence the voice maintains approximately the same range, and that this is the time to train it as a *child voice*.

The question now arises, why not use the girl's voice in choirs as well as the boy's?—and the answer is three-fold. In the first place, certain churches have always clung to the idea of the *male* choir, women being refused any participation in what originally was strictly a priestly office; in the second place, the girl arrives at the age of puberty somewhat earlier than the boy, and since her voice begins to change proportionately sooner, it is not serviceable for so long a period, and is therefore scarcely worth training as a child voice because of the short time during which it can be used in this capacity; and in the third place, the boy's voice is noticeably more brilliant between the ages of seven or eight and thirteen or fourteen, and is therefore actually more useful from the standpoint of both power and timbre. If it were not for such considerations as these, the choir of girls would doubtless be more common than the choir of boys, for girls are much more likely to be tractable at this age, and are in many ways far easier to deal with than boys.

At the age of six, the voices of boys and girls are essentially alike in timbre; but as the boy indulges in more vigorous play and work, and his muscles grow firmer and his whole body sturdier, the voice-producing mechanism too takes on these characteristics, and a group of thirty boys ten or twelve years old will actually produce tones that are considerably more brilliant than those made by a group of thirty girls of similar age.

THE COMPASS OF THE CHILD VOICE To the novice in handling children's voices, the statement that the typical voice of boys and girls about ten years of age easily reaches a″ and frequently b″ or c‴ will at first seem unbelievable. This is nevertheless the case, and the first thing to be learned by the trainer of

a boy choir is therefore to keep the boys singing high, beginning with the higher tones and vocalizing downward, instead of *vice versa*. The main reason for the necessity of this downward vocalization is what is known as the *movable break*. In an adult voice, the change from a low register to a higher one always takes place at approximately the same place in the scale; but the child's voice is immature, his vocal organs have not formed definitely established habits, and the chest register is often pushed upward to c″, d″, or even e″ This is practically always done in singing an ascending scale loudly, and the result is not only distressing to the listener, but ruinous to the voice. In former days this type of singing was common in our public schools, the result being that most boys honestly thought it impossible to sing higher than c″ or d″ this being the limit beyond which it was difficult to push the chest voice. The head voice was thus not used at all, and the singing of public school children in the past has in most cases been anything but satisfactory from the standpoint of tonal beauty. But most supervisors of music have now become somewhat familiar with the child voice, and are insisting upon high-pitched songs, light singing, and downward vocalization, these being the three indispensable factors in the proper training of children's voices. The result is that in many places school children are at the present time singing very well indeed, and the present growing tendency to encourage public performance by large groups of them makes available a new color to the composer of choral and orchestral music, and promises many a thrill to the concert-goer of the future.

It is the head register, or *thin* voice, that produces the pure, flute-like tones which are the essential charm of a boy choir, and if chest tones are to be employed at all, they must be made as nearly as possible as are the head tones, thus causing the voice to produce an approximately uniform timbre in the entire scale. This may be accomplished with a fair degree of ease by a strict adherence to the three principles of procedure mentioned in the above paragraph. In fact these three things are almost the beginning, middle, and end of child-voice training, and since they thus form the *sine qua non* of effective boy-choir singing, we shall emphasize them through reiteration.

1. The singing must be soft until the child has learned to produce tone correctly *as a habit*.

2. Downward vocalization should be employed in the early stages, so as to insure the use of the head voice.

3. The music should be high in range, in order that the voice may be given as favorable an opportunity as possible of producing its best tones.

When these principles are introduced in either a boy choir or a public school system, the effect will at first be disappointing, for the tone produced by the boy's head voice is so small and seems so insignificant as compared with the chest voice which he has probably been using, that he is apt to resent the instruction, and perhaps to feel that you are trying to make a baby, or worse yet, a girl, out of him! But he must be encouraged to persist, and after a few weeks or months of practice, the improvement in his singing will be so patent that there will probably be no further trouble.

THE LIFE OF THE BOY VOICE   Boys are admitted to male choirs at from seven or eight to ten or twelve years of age, but are often required to undergo a course of training lasting a year or more before being permitted to sing with the choir in public. For this reason, if for no other, the director of a boy choir must be a thoroughly qualified voice trainer. He, of course, takes no voice that is not reasonably good to start with, but after admitting a boy with a naturally good vocal organ it is his task so to train that voice as to enable it to withstand several hours of singing each day without injury and to produce tones of maximal beauty as a matter of habit. But if the choir leader is not a thoroughly qualified vocal instructor, or if he has erroneous ideals of what boy-voice tone should be, the result is frequently that the voice is overstrained and perhaps ruined; or else the singing is of an insipid, lifeless, "hooty" character, making one feel that an adult mixed choir is infinitely preferable to a boy choir.*

Adolescence begins at the age of thirteen or fourteen in boys, and with the growth of the rest of the body at this time, the vocal organs also resume their increase in size, the result being not only longer vocal cords and a correspondingly lower range of voice, but an absolute breaking down of the habits of singing that have been established, and frequently a temporary but almost total loss of control of the vocal organs. These changes sometimes take place as early as the thirteenth year, but on the other hand are frequently not noticeable until the boy is fifteen or sixteen, and there are on record instances of boys singing soprano in choirs until seventeen or even eighteen. The loss of control that accompanies the change of voice (with which we are all familiar because of having heard the queer alternations of squeaking and grumbling in which the adolescent boy so frequently indulges), is due to the fact that the larynx, vocal cords, *et cetera,* increase in size more rapidly than the muscles develop strength to manipulate them, and this rapid increase in the size of the parts (in boys a practical doubling in the length of the vocal cords) makes it incumbent upon the choir trainer to use extreme cau-

* Even when an ideal type of tone is secured, there is considerable difference of opinion as to whether the boy soprano is, all in all, as effective as the adult female voice. Many consider that the child is incapable of expressing a sufficient variety of emotions because of his lack of experience with life, and that the boy-soprano voice is therefore unsuited to the task assigned it, especially when the modern conception of religion is taken into consideration. But to settle this controversy is no part of our task, hence we shall not even express an opinion upon the matter.

tion in training the voices at this time, just as the employer of adolescent boys must use great care in setting them at any sort of a task involving heavy lifting or other kinds of strain. In the public schools, where no child is asked to sing more than ten or twelve minutes a day, no harm is likely to result; but in a choir which rehearses from one to two hours each day and frequently sings at a public service besides, it seems to be the consensus of opinion that the boy is taking a grave risk in continuing to sing while his voice is changing.* He is usually able to sing the high tones for a considerable period after the low ones begin to develop; but to continue singing the high tones is always attended with considerable danger, and many a voice has undoubtedly been ruined for after use by singing at this time. The reason for encouraging the boy to keep on singing is, of course, that the choirmaster, having trained a voice for a number of years, dislikes losing it when it is at the very acme of brilliancy. For this feeling he can hardly be blamed, for the most important condition of successful work by a male choir is probably permanency of membership; and the leader must exercise every wile to keep the boys in, once they have become useful members of the organization. But in justice to the boy's future, he ought probably in most cases to be dismissed from the choir when his voice begins to change.

Let us now summarize the advice given up to this point before going on to the consideration of our second problem:

 1. Have the boys sing in high range most of the time. The actual compass of the average choir boy's voice is probably g—c‴ but his best tones will be between e′ and g″. An occasional a″ or b″ or a d′ or c′ will do no harm, but the voice must not remain outside of the range e′—g″ for long at a time.

---

*Browne and Behnke, in *The Child's Voice*, p. 75, state in comment on a questionnaire sent out to a large number of choir trainers, singers, *et cetera*, that seventy-nine persons out of one hundred fifty-two stated positively that singing through the period of puberty "causes certain injury, deterioration, or ruin to the after voice." In the same book are found also (pp. 85 to 90) a series of extremely interesting comments on the choirmaster's temptation to use a voice after it begins to change.

2. Insist upon light singing until correct habits are established. There is a vast difference of opinion as to what light singing means, and we have no means of making the point clear except to say that at the outset of his career the boy can scarcely sing too softly. Later on, after correct habits are formed, the singing may, of course, be louder, but it should at no time be so loud as to sound strained.

3. Train the voice downward for some time before attempting upward vocalization.

4. Dismiss the boy from the choir when his voice begins to change, even if you need him and if he needs the money which he receives for singing.

THE BOY HIMSELF The second special problem mentioned at the beginning of this chapter is the management of the boys owning the voices which we have just been discussing; and this part of the choirmaster's task is considerably more complex, less amenable to codification, and requires infinitely more art for its successful prosecution. One may predict with reasonable certainty what a typical boy-voice will do as the result of certain treatment; but the wisest person can not foresee what the result will be when the boy himself is subjected to any specified kind of handling. As a matter of fact, there is no such thing as a *typical* boy, and even if there were, our knowledge of boy nature in general has been, at least up to comparatively recent times, so slight that it has been impossible to give directions as to his management.

HOW TO HANDLE BOYS In general, that choir director will succeed best in keeping his boys in the choir and in getting them to do good work, who, other things being equal, keeps on the best terms with them personally. Our advice is, therefore, that the prospective director of a choir of boys find out just as much as possible about the likes and dislikes, the predilections and the prejudices of pre-adolescent boys, and especially that he investigate ways and means of getting on good terms with them. He will find that most boys are intensely active at this stage, for their

bodies are not growing very much, and there is therefore a large amount of superfluous energy.   This activity
on their part is perfectly natural and indeed wholly com-
mendable; and yet it will be very likely to get the boy
into trouble unless some one is at hand to guide his
energy into useful channels.   This does not necessarily
mean making him do things that he does not like to
do; on the contrary, it frequently involves helping him
to do better, something that he already has a taste for
doing.   Space does not permit details; but if the reader
will investigate the Boy Scout movement, the supervised
playground .idea, and the development of school ath-
letics, as well as the introduction of manual training of
various sorts, trips to museums of natural history,
zoölogical and botanical gardens, *et cetera*, school
"hikes" and other excursions, and similar activities
that now constitute a part of the regular school work in
many of our modern educational institutions, he will
find innumerable applications of the idea that we are
presenting; and he will perhaps be surprised to discover
that the boy of today *likes* to go to school; that he applies at home many of the things that he learns there,
and that he frequently regards some teacher as his best
friend instead of as an arch enemy, as formerly.   These
desirable changes have not taken place in all schools by
any means, but the results of their introduction have
been so significant that a constantly increasing number
of schools are adopting them; and public school education is to mean infinitely more in the future than it has
in the past because we are seeing the necessity of looking at things through the eyes of the pupil, and especially
from the standpoint of his life outside of and after leaving the school.   Let the choir trainer learn a lesson
from the public school teacher, and let him not consider
the boy to be vicious just because he is lively, and let
him not try to repress the activity but rather let him
train it into useful channels.   Above all, let him not

fail to take into consideration the boy's viewpoint, always treating his singers in such a way that they will feel that he is "playing fair." It has been found that if boys are given a large share in their own government, they are not only far easier to manage at the time, but grow enormously in maturity of social ideals, and are apt to become much more useful citizens because of such growth. Placing responsibility upon the boys involves trusting them, of course, but it has been found that when the matter has been presented fairly and supervised skilfully, they have always risen to the responsibility placed upon their shoulders. We therefore recommend that self-government be inaugurated in the boy choir, that the boys be allowed to elect officers out of their own ranks, and that the rules and regulations be worked out largely by the members themselves with a minimum of assistance from the choirmaster.

Let us not make the serious mistake of supposing that in order to get on the good side of boys we must make their work easy. Football is not easy, but it is extremely popular! It is the motive rather than the intrinsic difficulty of the task that makes the difference. The thing needed by the choir director is a combination of firmness (but not crossness) with the play spirit. Let him give definite directions, and let these directions be given with such decision that there will never be any doubt as to whether they are to be obeyed; but let him always treat the boys courteously and pleasantly, and let him always convey the idea that he is not only *fair* in his attitude toward them, but that he is attempting to be *friendly* as well.

Work the boys hard for a half hour or so, therefore, and then stop for five minutes and join them in a game of leapfrog, if that is the order of the day. If they invite you to go with them on a hike or picnic, refuse at your peril; and if you happen to be out on the ball ground when one side is short a player, do not be afraid of losing your dignity, but jump at the chance of taking a hand in the game. Some one has said that "familiarity breeds contempt, only if one of the persons be contemptible," and this dictum might well be applied to the management of the boy choir. On the other hand, it is absolutely necessary to maintain discipline in the choir rehearsal, and it is also necessary to arouse in the boys a mental attitude that will cause them to do efficient work and to conduct themselves in a quiet and reverent manner during the church service; hence the necessity for rules and regulations and for punishments of various kinds. But the two things that we have been outlining are entirely compatible, and the choir director who plays with the boys and is hailed by them as a good fellow will on the whole have far less trouble than he who holds himself aloof and tries to reign as a despot over his little kingdom.

REMUNERATION *ET CETERA* In conclusion, a word should perhaps be added about various plans of remunerating the boys for their singing. In some large churches and cathedrals a choir-school is maintained and the boys receive food, clothing, shelter, and education in return for their services; but this entails a very heavy expense, and in most smaller churches the boys are paid a certain amount for each rehearsal and service, or possibly a lump sum per week. The amount received by each boy depends upon his voice, his experience, his attitude toward the work, *et cetera*, in other words, upon his usefulness as a member of the choir. Attempts have often been made to organize a boy choir on the volunteer basis, but this plan has not usually proved to be successful, and is not advocated.

When the boys live in their own homes and there are Sunday services only, the usual plan is to have them meet for about two rehearsals each week by themselves, with a third rehearsal for the full choir. Often the men have a separate practice also, especially if they are not good readers.

If the organization is to be permanent, it will be necessary to be constantly on the lookout for new voices, these being trained partly by themselves and partly by singing with the others at the rehearsals through the period of weeks or months before they are permitted to take part in the public services. In this way the changing voices that drop out are constantly being replaced by newly trained younger boys, and the number in the chorus is kept fairly constant.

CHAPTER XIII

THE CONDUCTOR AS VOICE TRAINER

THE CONDUCTOR'S NEED OF VOCAL TRAINING
Correct voice placement, the full use of the resonance cavities, good habits of breathing, and other details connected with what is commonly termed *voice culture*, cannot be taught by correspondence; neither can the conductor be made an efficient voice trainer by reading books. But so many choral conductors are failing to secure adequate results from their choruses because of their ignorance of even the fundamentals of singing, that it has been thought best to include a brief presentation of a few of the most important matters with which the conductor ought to be acquainted. In discussing these things it will only be possible for us to present to the student of conducting the problems involved, leaving their actual working out to each individual. The chief difficulty in connection with the whole matter arises from the fact that the conductor needs in his work certain qualities of musicianship that are more apt to result from instrumental than from vocal training, the education of the instrumentalist usually emphasizing harmony, ear-training, form, and in general, the intellectual aspect of music; while that of the vocalist too often entirely leaves out this invaluable type of training, dealing only with voice culture and in general the interpretative side of music study. The vocalist who attempts to conduct is therefore frequently criticized for his lack of what is called "solid musical training"; but the instrumentalist-conductor as often fails to get adequate results in working with singers because of his utter ignorance of vocal procedure; and this latter type of failure is probably as productive of poor choral singing as the former. This

chapter is, of course, written especially for the instrumentalist, and our advice to him is not merely to read
books about singing, but to study singing itself, whether
he is interested in cultivating his own voice for solo purposes or not. It might be remarked in this connection
that aside from the considerations that we have been
naming, the conductor who can sing a phrase to his
orchestra or chorus and thus show by imitation exactly
what shading, *et cetera*, he wishes, has an enormous advantage over him who can only convey his ideas by means of
words.

PROPER   Probably the first thing about singing to
BREATHING   be learned by the student of conducting is
                    that good voice production depends upon
using the full capacity of the lungs instead of merely the
upper portion. Hence the necessity of holding the body
easily erect as a matter of habit, with chest up, and with
the diaphragm alternately pushing the viscera away in
order to enable the lungs to expand downward, and then
allowing the parts to come back into place again, as the
air is in turn expelled from the lungs. By practising
deep breathing in this way the actual capacity of the
lungs may be considerably increased, and breathing
exercises have therefore always formed part of the rou-
tine imposed upon the vocal student. A deep breath
involves, then, a pushing down of the diaphragm and
a pushing out of the lower ribs, and not merely an expansion of the upper part of the chest. The singer
must form the habit of breathing in this way at all
times. To test breathing, the singer may place the
hands about the waist on the sides of the thorax (fingers
toward the front, thumbs toward the back) and see
whether there is good side expansion of the ribs in inhal-
ing, and whether in taking breath the abdomen swells
out, receding as the air is expelled. We have always felt
that a few minutes spent at each chorus rehearsal in

deep breathing and in vocalizing would more than justify the time taken from practising music; but such exercises should not be undertaken unless the conductor understands singing and knows exactly what their purpose is.

It is important that the conductor should understand the difference between the use of the singer's *full breath* which we have been describing, and his *half breath*. The full breath is taken at punctuation marks of greater value, at long rests, before long sustained tones, and, in solo singing, before long trills or cadenzas. The half breath is usually taken at the lesser punctuation marks and at short rests, when it is necessary to replenish the supply of air in as short a time as possible, in order not to interrupt the *legato* any more than is absolutely necessary.

BREATH CONTROL The next point to be noted is that, having provided as large a supply of air as possible every particle of it must now be made use of in producing tone; in the first place, in order that no breath may be wasted, and in the second place, in order that the purity of the tone may not be marred by non-vocalized escaping breath. This implies absolute breath control, and the skilful singer is able to render incredibly long phrases in one breath, not so much because his lungs have more capacity, but because every atom of breath actually functions in producing vocal tone. And because of the fact that no breath escapes without setting the cords in vibration, the tone is clear, and not "breathy." The secret of expressive singing in sustained melody is absolutely steady tone combined with a perfect *legato*, and neither of these desirable things can be achieved without perfect breath control, this matter applying to choral singing as forcefully as it does to solo work.

RESONANCE   The next point to be noted is that the carrying power and quality of a voice depend far more upon the use made of the resonance cavities than upon the violence with which the vocal cords vibrate. Every musical instrument involves, in its production of tone, a combination of three elements:

1. The vibrating body.

2. The force which sets the body in vibration.

3. The reinforcing medium (the sound board of a piano, the body of a violin, *et cetera*.)

In the case of the human voice, the vocal cords (or, as they might more properly be termed, the vocal *bands*) constitute the vibrating body; the air expelled from the lungs is the force which sets the cords in vibration; and the cavities of the mouth, nose, and to a lesser extent, of the remainder of the head and even of the chest, are the reinforcing medium—the resonator. A small voice cannot of course be made into a large one; but by improving its placement, and particularly by reinforcing it with as much resonance power as possible, it may be caused to fill even a large auditorium. This involves such details as keeping the tongue down, allowing part of the air to pass through the nose, focusing the tone against the roof of the mouth just back of the teeth, opening the mouth exactly the right distance, forming the lips in just the right way, *et cetera*. The result is that instead of sounding as though it came from the throat, the tone apparently comes from the upper part of the mouth just back of the teeth; and instead of seeming to be forced out, it appears to flow or float out without the slightest effort on the part of the singer. A forced or squeezed-out tone is always bad—bad for the voice and bad for the ear of the listener!

THE VOWEL IN   Another point to be noted by the con-
SINGING   ductor is that one sings upon vowels and not upon consonants; that most of the consonants are in fact merely devices for interrupt-

ing the vowel sounds in various ways; and that good tone depends largely upon the ability of the singer to select the best of several different sounds of the vowel and to hold this sound without any change in quality during the entire time that the tone is prolonged. It is comparatively easy to make a good tone with some vowels, but extremely difficult with others, and it is the singer's task so to modify the vowel that is unfavorable as to make it easier to produce good tone in using it. But while thus modifying the actual vowel sound, the integrity of the vowel must at least be sufficiently pre- served to enable the listener to understand what vowel is being sung. All this is particularly difficult in singing loudly, and it is largely for this reason that the vocal student is required by his teacher to practise softly so much of the time. Some vowels have two parts (*e.g.*, i $=$ ä $+$ ē), and here it is the singer's task to sustain the part upon which the better tone can be made, sound- ing the other part only long enough to produce a correct total effect.

CONSONANTS   As noted above, the consonants are in general merely devices for cutting off the flow of vowel sound in various ways, and one of the most difficult problems confronting the singer in his public performances is to articulate the consonants so skilfully that the words shall be easy to follow by the audience, and at the same time to keep the vowel sounds so pure and their flow so uninterrupted that the singing may be perfect in its tone quality and in its *legato*. It is because this matter presents great difficulty that the words of the singer with a good *legato* can so seldom be under- stood, while the declamatory vocalist who presents his words faultlessly is apt to sing with no *legato* at all. The problem is not insoluble, but its solution can only be accomplished through years of study under expert guidance. Vocal teachers in general will probably disagree with us; but it is our opinion that in choral performance at least, the *tone* rather than the *words* should be sacrificed if one or the other has to give way, and the choral conductor is therefore advised to study the use of the consonants most carefully, and to find out how to make use of every means of securing well enunciated words from his body of singers.

RELAXATION   The next point to be noted is the importance of what vocal teachers refer to as the "movable lower jaw," this, of course, implying absolute (but controlled) relaxation of all muscles used in singing. Without relaxation of this sort, the tone is very likely to be badly placed, the sound seeming to come from the throat, and the whole effect being that of tone squeezed out or forced out instead of tone flowing or floating out, as described in a previous paragraph. This difficulty is, of course, most obvious in singing the higher tones; and one remedy within the reach of the choral conductor is to test all voices carefully and not to allow anyone to sing a part that is obviously too high. But in addition to this general treatment of the matter, it will often be possible for the director to urge upon his chorus the necessity of relaxation in producing tone, thus reminding those who tighten up unconsciously that they are not singing properly, and conveying to those who are ignorant of the matter at least a hint regarding a better use of their voices.

VOCAL   A vocal register has been defined as "a
REGISTERS   series of tones produced by the same mechanism." This means that in beginning with the lowest tone of the voice and ascending the scale, one comes to a point where before going on to the next scale-tone, a readjustment of the vocal organs is necessary, this change in the action of the larynx and vocal cords being *felt* by the singer and *heard* by the

listener. The point at which the readjustment takes place, *i.e.*, the place where the voice goes from one register into another, is called the *break;* and one of the things the voice trainer tries to do for each pupil is to teach him to pass so skilfully from one register to another that these breaks will not be noticeable to the hearer—the voice eventually sounding an even scale from its lowest to its highest tone. There is considerable difference of opinion as to the number of registers existing in any one voice, but perhaps the majority of writers incline to the view that there are three: the chest or lower, the thin or middle, and the small or head. It should be noted, however, that the readjustment in the action of the vocal cords referred to above probably takes place only when passing from the lowest register to the next higher one, and that such changes in action as occur at other points are more or less indefinite and possibly even somewhat imaginary. Authorities differ as to just what the change in mechanism is in passing from the chest register to the middle one; but the most plausible explanation seems to be that in the lowest register, the change in pitch from a lower tone to the next higher one is accomplished at least partly by *stretching* the vocal bands more tightly, and that when the limit of this stretching process has been reached, the cords relax slightly, and from this point on each higher tone is made by *shortening* the vibrating portion of the cords; in other words, by decreasing the length of the glottis (the aperture between the vocal cords). This point may become clearer if we compare the process with tuning a violin string. The string may be a third or a fourth below its normal pitch when the violinist begins to tune his instrument, but by turning the peg and thus stretching the string tighter and tighter, the tone is raised by small degrees until the string gives forth the pitch that it is supposed to sound. But this same string may now be made to play higher and higher pitches by pressing it against the fingerboard, thus shortening the vibrating portion more and more. The tuning process may be said to compare roughly with the mechanism of the chest register of the human voice; while the shortening of the string by pressing it against the fingerboard is somewhat analogous to what takes place in the higher registers of the voice.

We have now enumerated what seem to us to be the most essential matters connected with vocal procedure; and if to such information as is contained in the foregoing paragraphs the conductor adds the knowledge that the *messa di voce* (a beautiful vocal effect produced by swelling a tone from soft to loud and then back again) is to be produced by increase and decrease of breath pressure and not by a greater or lesser amount of straining of the throat muscles; that *portamento* (gliding by infinitely small degrees in pitch from one tone to another), although a valuable and entirely legitimate expressional effect when used occasionally in a passage where its employment is appropriate, may be over-used to such an extent as to result in a slovenly, vulgar, and altogether objectionable style of singing; and that whereas the *vibrato* may imbue with virility and warmth an otherwise cold, dead tone and if skilfully and judiciously used may add greatly to the color and vitality of the singing, the *tremolo* is on the other hand a destroyer of pitch accuracy, a despoiler of vocal idealism, and an abhorrence to the listener; if our conductor knows these and other similar facts about singing, then he will not run quite so great a risk of making himself ridiculous in the eyes of the singers whom he is conducting as has sometimes been the case when instrumentalists have assumed control of vocal forces. But let us emphasize again the fact that these things cannot be learned from a book, but must be acquired through self-activity, *i.e.*, by actual experience in singing; hence the importance of vocal study on the part of the prospective choral conductor.

In conclusion, let us enumerate the main points involved in what is called good singing—these points applying to choral music as directly as to solo performance.

1. The intonation must be perfect; *i.e.*, the tones produced must be neither sharp nor flat, but exactly true to pitch.

2. The tone must be attacked and released exactly at the right pitch; *i.e.*, the voice must not begin on some indefinite lower tone and slide up, or on a higher tone and slide down, but must begin on precisely the right pitch.

3. The tone must be absolutely steady, and there must be no wavering, no *tremolo*, no uncertainty. This implies perfect breath control.

4. The tones must follow one another without break, unless the character of the music demands detached effects; in other words, there must be a perfect *legato*. The tones must also follow each other cleanly, unless the character of the music makes the use of *portamento* desirable.

5. The singer must feel the mood of each song, and must sing as he feels, if he is to perform with real expression. This is a much more vital matter in song interpretation than the mere mechanical observation of *tempo* and *dynamic* indications.

6. The text must be enunciated with sufficient clarity to enable the audience to catch at least the most important ideas presented. This involves not only the *complete* pronunciation of each syllable instead of the slovenly half-pronunciation so commonly heard; but implies as well that the sounds be formed well forward in the mouth instead of back in the throat.

7. There must be tasteful shading, including the artistic use of *messa di voce* and other subtle expressional devices.

If the singing of a soloist or a chorus can meet the test of these requirements, the singing may be called good.

CHAPTER XIV

THE ART OF PROGRAM MAKING

THE PROBLEM
STATED
In constructing a concert program for either a solo or an ensemble performance, and in the case of both vocal and instrumental music, at least five important points must be taken into consideration:

1. Variety.
2. Unity.
3. Effective arrangement.
4. Appropriate length.
5. Adaptability to audience.

VARIETY We have given variety first place advisedly; for it is by changing the style and particularly through varying the emotional quality of the selections that the conductor or performer will find it most easy to hold the attention and interest of the audience. In these days the matter of keeping an audience interested presents far greater difficulty than formerly, for our audiences are now much more accustomed to hearing good music than they used to be, and a performance that is moderately good and that would probably have held the attention from beginning to end in the olden days will now often be received with yawning, coughing, whispering, early leaving, and a spirit of uneasiness permeating the entire audience, especially during the latter part of the program. The change of etiquette brought about by the phenomenal popularization of the moving picture theater has doubtless had something to do with this change in the attitude of our audiences; the spread of musical knowledge and the far greater intelligence concerning musical performance manifested by the average audience of today as compared with that of fifty years ago is also partly responsible; but the brunt of the charge must be borne by our habitual attitude of nervous hurry, our impatience with slow processes of any kind, and the demand for constant change of sensation that is coming to characterize Americans of all ages and classes. It is doubtless unfortunate that conditions are as they are; but since the attitude of our audiences has admittedly undergone a decided change, it behooves the program maker to face conditions as they actually exist, rather than to pretend that they are as he should like them to be. Since our audiences are harder to hold now than formerly, and since our first-class performers (except possibly in the case of orchestral music) are probably not greatly above the level of the first-class performers of a generation ago (although larger in number), it will be necessary to keep the listener interested by employing methods of program making, which, although they have always been not only entirely legitimate but highly desirable, are now absolutely necessary. As stated above, the obvious way to help our audience to listen to an entire concert is to provide variety of material—a heavy number followed by a light one; a slow, flowing *adagio* by a bright snappy *scherzo;* a tragic and emotionally taxing song like the *Erl-King* by a sunny and optimistic lyric; a song or a group of songs in major possibly relieved by one in minor; a coloratura aria by a song in cantabile style; a group of songs in French by a group in English; a composition in severe classic style by one of romantic tendency, *et cetera.* These contrasting elements are not, of course, to be introduced exactly as they are here listed, and this series of possible contrasts is cited rather to give the amateur maker of programs an idea of what is meant by contrast rather than to lay down rules to be followed in the actual construction of programs.

UNITY   But while contrast is necessary to keep the audience from becoming bored or weary, there must not be so much variety that a lack of unity is felt in the program as a whole.   It must be constructed like a symphony—out of material that has variety and yet that all belongs together.   In other words, the program, like a musical composition, must achieve *unity in variety;* and this is the second main problem confronting the conductor or performer who is planning a concert.   It is impossible to give specific directions as to how unity is to be secured, for this is a matter to be determined almost wholly upon the basis of taste, and taste is not subjectable to codification.   The most that we can do for the amateur at this point, as at so many others, is to set before him the main problem involved, and in constructing a program, this is undoubtedly to provide variety of material and yet to select numbers that go well together and seem to cohere as a unified group.

LENGTH   Our third question in making a program of musical works is, how long shall it be? The answer is, "It depends upon the quality of the audience." An audience composed largely of trained concert-goers, many of whom are themselves musicians, can listen to a program composed of interesting works and presented by a first-rate artist even though it extends through a period of two and a half hours, although on general prin ciples a two-hour program is probably long enough. But one made up mostly of people who have had very little musical training, who read little except the daily newspaper and the lightest sort of fiction, and whose chief amusement is probably attendance upon the picture show,—such an audience must not be expected to listen to a program that is either too heavy or too long; and our judgment is that for such a group a program an hour and a half long is probably more suitable than one of two or two and a half hours.   Our feeling is, furthermore, that the "tired business man" would not object so strenuously to attending the serious musical performances to which his wife urges him to go if some of these matters were considered more carefully by the artist in planning the program! But here again, of course, we have a matter which depends altogether upon the kind of music presented, whether the entire program is given by one artist or whether there are several performers, whether the whole program is of one kind of music or whether there is variety of voice and instrument, whether the performers are amateurs or professionals, and upon whether the performer is an artist of the first rank and is able by his perfection of technique, his beauty of tone, and his emotional verve, to hold his audience spellbound for an indefinite length of time, or whether he belongs to the second or third rank of performers and is able to arouse only an average amount of interest. Our purpose in including a discussion of the matter is principally in order that we may have an opportunity of warning the amateur conductor not to cause an audience which would probably give favorable consideration to a short program, to become weary and critical by compelling them to sit through too long a performance. This is particularly true in the case of amateur performance; and since this book is written chiefly for the amateur director, it may not be out of order to advise him at this point to plan programs not more than an hour or an hour and a quarter long, at first. It is far better to have the audience leaving the auditorium wishing the program had been longer than to have them grumbling because it is too long.

ADAPTABILITY Our fourth problem has already been
TO AUDIENCES presented in discussing the other three, for it is because of the necessity of adapting the performance to the audience that we have

insisted upon variety, unity, and reasonable length. Many a concert has turned out to be an utter fiasco because of failure on the part of the program maker to consider the type of people who were to listen to it; and although on such occasions it is customary for the performer to ascribe his failure to the stupidity of the audience, it must nevertheless be acknowledged that the fault is more commonly to be laid at the door of the one who planned the event. A program composed of two symphonies and an overture or two, or of two or three Beethoven sonatas, is not a suitable meal for the conglomerate crowd comprising the "average audience"; indeed it is doubtful whether in general it is the best kind of diet for any group of listeners. Here again we cannot give specific directions, since conditions vary greatly, and we must content ourselves once more with having opened up the problem for thought and discussion.

EFFECTIVE ARRANGEMENT   Having selected musical material that is varied in content and yet appropriate for performance upon the same program; having taken into consideration what kind of music is adapted to our audience and how much of it they will probably be able to listen to without becoming weary; our final problem will now be so to arrange the numbers that each one will be presented at the point in the program where it will be likely to be most favorably received, and will make the most lasting impression upon the auditors.

In general, of course, the heavier part of the program should usually come in the first half and the lighter part in the second, for the simple reason that it is at the beginning that our minds and bodies are fresh and unwearied, and since we are able to give closer attention at that time we should accordingly be supplied with the more strenuous music when we are best able to digest it. But although this is doubtless true in most cases, we have often noticed that audiences are restless during the first part of the concert, and frequently do not get "warmed up" to the point of giving close attention to the performance until ten or fifteen minutes after the program begins, and sometimes not until the second half has been reached. For this reason, and also to cover the distraction arising from the entrance of the ubiquitous late-comer, it seems best to us that some shorter and lighter work be placed at the very beginning of the program—possibly an overture, in the case of a symphony concert. The phenomenon here alluded to has an exact parallel in the church service. When we enter the church, we are thinking about all sorts of things connected with our daily life, and it takes us some little time to forget these extraneous matters and adjust ourselves to the spirit of a church service, and particularly to get into the appropriate mood for listening to a sermon. The organ prelude and other preliminary parts of the service have as their partial function, at least, the transference of our thoughts and attitudes from their former chaotic and egoistic state to one more appropriate to the demands of the more serious part of the service to follow. Somewhat the same sort of thing is found in the case of the majority of people who go to a concert hall for an evening's performance, and although the end to be attained is of course altogether different, yet the method should probably be somewhat the same. Our feeling is therefore that there ought usually to be some comparatively light number at the beginning of the concert program in order that we may be assisted in getting into the listening mood before the heavier works are presented. On the other hand, an artist often plunges into a difficult composition at the very beginning of the concert, and by his marvelous technique or his tremendous emotional vitality sweeps his audience immediately into an attitude of rapt attention; all of which proves again that art is intangible, subtle, and ever-vary-ing—as we stated at the beginning.

THE IMPORTANCE
OF SMALL DETAILS   In concluding our very brief state-ment of program-making, it may be well to mention the fact that small details often have a good deal to do with the failure of audiences to follow the program with as keen attention as might be desired. These details are often overlooked or disdained merely because they seem too trifling to make it worth the artist's while to notice them; but by seeing to it that the concert hall is well warmed (or well cooled), that it is well lighted and well ventilated; that the doors are closed when the first number begins, and that no one is allowed to enter during the performance of any number; that there are no long waits either at the beginning or between numbers; that unnecessary street and other outside noises are stopped or shut out so far as practicable; and that the printed program (if it has more than one sheet) is so arranged that the pages do not have to be turned while compositions are being performed —by providing in advance for someone who will see to all these little matters, the artist may often be rewarded by a fine type of concentrated attention which would not be possible if the minds of the individuals comprising the audience were being distracted by these other things.

The printer too bears no small responsibility in this matter of having an audience follow a program with un-diminished attention from beginning to end, and there is no doubt that the tastefully printed page (and par-ticularly if there are explanatory remarks concerning the composer, style, meaning of the composition, *et cetera*) will usually be followed with much keener attention than one the parts of which have merely been thrown to-gether. The reason for this we shall leave for some one else to discuss—possibly some writer of the future upon "the psychology of the printed page."

CHAPTER XV

Conductor and Accompanist

NECESSITY OF
CORDIAL
RELATION
In chorus directing, it is of the utmost importance that conductor and accompanist not only understand one another thoroughly, but that the relationship between them be so sympathetic, so cordial, that there may never be even a hint of non-unity in the ensemble. The unskilful or unsympathetic accompanist may utterly ruin the effect of the most capable conducting; and the worst of it is that if the accompanist is lacking in cordiality toward the conductor, he can work his mischief so subtly as to make it appear to all concerned as if the conductor himself were to blame for the ununified attacks and ragged rhythms.*

CHOOSING THE
ACCOMPANIST
In order to obviate the disadvantages that are likely to arise from having a poor accompanist, the conductor must exercise the greatest care in choosing his coworker. Unless he knows of some one concerning whose ability there is no question, the best plan is probably to have several candidates compete for the position; and in this case, the points to be especially watched for are as follows:

1. Adequate technique.
2. Good reading ability.
3. Sympathetic response to vocal *nuance.*
4. Willingness to cooperate and to accept suggestions.

* On the other hand, the conductor sometimes shifts the responsibility for mishaps to the accompanist when the latter is in no wise to blame, as, *e.g.*, when the organ ciphers or a page does not turn properly.

Of these four, the last two are by no means the least important; and sometimes it is better to choose the person who has less skill in reading or technique but who has sufficient innate musical feeling to enable him not only to follow a soloist's voice or a conductor's beat intelligently, but even to anticipate the dynamic and tempo changes made by singer or conductor.

The minds of conductor and accompanist must work as one. In stopping his chorus for a correction, it should be possible for the conductor to assume that the accompanist has followed him so carefully and is in such close musical rapport with him that, before the conductor speaks, the accompanist has already found the badly executed passage, and the instant the conductor cites page and score, is ready to play the phrase or interval that was wrongly rendered. The same sort of thing ought of course to take place whenever there is a change of tempo, and it is to be noted that in all these cases the accompanist must make a *musical* response to the conductor's interpretation, and not merely an *obedient* one.

COURTEOUS TREATMENT NECESSARY   Having chosen the best available person to do the accompanying, the next thing in order will be to treat the accompanist in such a way that he will always do his best and be a real help in causing the chorus to produce effective results. Next to the conductor, the accompanist is undoubtedly the most important factor in producing fine choral singing; hence our reference to the accompanist as the conductor's *coworker*. The first thing to note in connection with getting the best possible help from the accompanist is that he shall always be treated in a pleasant, courteous way, and the conductor must learn at the very outset not to expect impossible things from him; not to blame him for things that may go wrong when some one else is really responsible; and in general, to do his utmost to bring about and to maintain friendly, pleasant relations. This will mean a smile of approval when the accompanist has done particularly well; it may involve publicly sharing honors with him after a well rendered performance; and it certainly implies a receptive attitude on the conductor's part if the accompanist is sufficiently interested to make occasional suggestions about the rendition of the music.

If you as conductor find it necessary to make criticisms or suggestions to the accompanist, do this privately, not in the presence of the chorus. Much of the sting of a criticism frequently results from the fact that others have heard it, and very often if the matter is brought up with the utmost frankness in a private interview, no bad blood will result, but if a quarter as much be said in the presence of others, a rankling wound may remain which will make it extremely difficult for the conductor and accompanist to do good musical work together thenceforth.

NECESSITY OF PROVIDING THE MUSIC IN ADVANCE One of the best ways to save time at the rehearsal is to provide the accompanist with the music in advance. Even a skilful reader will do more intelligent work the first time a composition is taken up if he has had an opportunity to go through it beforehand. This may involve considerable trouble on the conductor's part, but his effort will be well rewarded in the much more effective support that the accompanist will be able to furnish if he has had an opportunity to look over the music. When the accompanist is not a good reader, it is, of course, absolutely imperative that he not only be given an opportunity to study the score in advance, but that he be *required* to do so. If in such a case the conductor does not see to it that a copy of the music is placed in the accompanist's hands several days before each rehearsal, he will simply be digging his own grave, figuratively speaking, and will have no one but himself to blame for the poor results that are bound to follow.

ORGAN
ACCOMPANYING
If the accompaniments are played on the organ, the conductor will need to take into consideration the fact that preparing and manipulating stops, pistons, and combination pedals takes time, and he will therefore not expect the organist to be ready to begin to play the instant he takes his place on the bench; neither will he be unreasonable enough to assume that the organist ought to be ready to pass from one number to another (*e.g.*, from a solo accompaniment to a chorus) without being given a reasonable amount of time for arranging the organ. The fact that in such a case the accompanist has been working continuously, whereas the director has had an opportunity of resting during the solo number, ought also to be taken into consideration; and it may not be unreasonable for the organist to wish for a moment's pause in order that he may adjust his mental attitude from that demanded by the preceding number to that which is appropriate to the number to follow. All this is especially to be noted in performances of sacred music, in which no time is taken between the numbers for applause. In any case, the least the conductor can do is to watch for the organist to look up after he has prepared the organ, and then to signal him pleasantly with a nod and a smile that he is ready to go on with the next number. This will not only insure complete preparedness of the organ, but will help "oil the machinery" and keep relations pleasant.

The conductor of a church choir should remember that the organist has probably studied and is familiar with the dynamic resources of his instrument to a much greater extent than the conductor; and that many times the organist is not depending upon his *ear* in deciding the amount of organ needed, so much as upon his *knowledge* of what the total effect will be in the auditorium. It is frequently impossible to tell from the choir loft how loud or how soft the sound of the organ is in the body of the house. The conductor, not knowing the dynamic values of the various stop combinations as well as the organist, must not presume to criticize the latter for playing too loudly or too softly unless he has gone down into the auditorium to judge the effect there. Even this is not an absolute guide, for the balance is very likely to be different when the auditorium is full of people from what it was when empty. Moreover, the amount of choral tone frequently increases greatly under the stimulus of public performance. All in all, therefore, a good organist should be permitted to use his own judgment in this matter. In any case, do not resort to conspicuous gestures to let him know that there is too much or too little organ. He has probably discovered it as soon as you have, and will add or subtract as soon as it can be done without making an inartistic break in the dynamic continuity of the accompaniment. If a signal becomes absolutely necessary, make it as inconspicuously as possible.

ACCOMPANIST MUST SEE DIRECTOR   We have previously stressed the fact that the conductor must stand so that his beat may be easily seen by all performers; and this matter is of the utmost importance in connection with the accompanist. He must be able to see you *easily* if he is to follow your beat accurately; further, he should be able to see your face as well as your baton, if a really sympathetic musical relationship is to exist. This may appear to be a small point, but its non-observance is responsible for many poor attacks and for much "dragging" and "running away" on the part of accompanists.

The sum and substance of the whole matter may be epitomized in the advice, "Be courteous, considerate, and sensible in dealing with your accompanist and verily thou shalt receive thy reward!"

CHAPTER XVI

Efficiency in the Rehearsal

ORGANIZING ABILITY
NEEDED TO AVOID
WASTING TIME
Having now reviewed the various essentials in conducting from the standpoint of public performance, we wish emphatically to state our conviction that in many cases both choruses and orchestras have been short-lived, being abandoned after a season or two of more or less unsatisfactory work, directly as a result of the inefficient methods used by the conductor in the rehearsal. In an earlier chapter (p. 18) we noted that the successful conductor of the present day must possess a personality combining traits almost opposite in their nature; *viz.*, *artistry* and *organizing ability*. We were referring at that time to business sense in general as needed by the conductor in selecting works to be performed, deciding upon the place, duration, and number of rehearsal periods, engaging artists to assist in the public performances, and in general, seeing to it that the business details of the organization are attended to in an efficient manner. But such organizing ability is needed most of all in planning and conducting the rehearsal, and there is no doubt that mediocre results at the public performance and not infrequently the actual breaking up of amateur organizations may be traced more often to the inability of the conductor to make the best use of his time in the always inadequate rehearsal hour than to any other source. It is for this reason that we have thought best to devote an entire chapter to a discussion of what might be termed "The Technique of the Rehearsal."

EFFICIENCY NOT
A DESTROYER OF
IDEALISM
The word *efficiency* has been used so frequently in recent years that it has come to be in almost as bad odor as the word *artistic*, as employed by the would-be critic of esthetic effects. This antipathy to the word is perhaps most pronounced on the part of the artist, and there has been a well-defined feeling on the part of a good many of us that efficiency and advancement in art appreciation do not perhaps go hand-in-hand as much as might be desired. Granting the validity of this criticism of efficiency as a national ideal, it must nevertheless be evident that the artist has in the past been far too little concerned with life's business affairs, and that both he and his family on the one hand, and those having business relations with him on the other would be far better off if the artist would cultivate a more businesslike attitude in his relationships with the rest of the world. However this may be in general, it is certain that the conductor of the present must take more definitely into consideration what is going on outside the world of art; must recognize the fact that this is now a busy world and that there are a great many interesting things to do and a great many more distractions and amusements than there were a half-century ago; and that if the members of a chorus or orchestra (particularly in the case of an amateur society) are to continue to attend rehearsals regularly and to keep up their enthusiasm for the work of the organization, the conductor must see to it that something tangible is accomplished not only during each season, but in each and every practice hour, and that regular attendance at the rehearsals does not cause the members to feel that they are wasting time and energy.

This is, after all, the essence of scientific management— to accomplish some desired result without any waste moves and without squandering valuable material; and surely no artistic loss will be involved if efficiency of this type is applied to conducting a musical rehearsal. On the contrary, the application of such methods will enable the conductor to secure a much higher degree of artistry in the public performance because, by avoiding any waste of time in rehearsing, he will be able to put the musicians through the music more often, and thus not only arouse greater confidence on their part, but be enabled to emphasize more strongly the interpretative, the artistic aspect of the music. Most of the rehearsal hour is often spent in drilling upon mere *correctness* of tone and rhythm, especially in the case of amateur organizations.

In order to make these matters as concrete and practical as possible, we shall give in the remainder of this chapter a series of somewhat unrelated suggestions about conducting an ensemble rehearsal, trusting that the reader will forgive the didactic (and possibly pedantic) language in which they are couched.

PLANNING   Do not make the mistake of attempting
THE REHEARSAL   to study your score at the same time
                that your singers or players are learning it. Study your music exhaustively beforehand so that at the rehearsal you may know definitely just what you are going to do with each selection and may be able to give pointed directions as to its rendition. This will enable you to look at your performers most of the time, and the freedom from the score thus allowed will make your conducting very much more effective and will enable you to stir your singers out of their state of inertia very much more quickly. Weingartner, in writing upon this point (with especial reference to the public performance) says:* "He should know it [the score] so thoroughly that during the performance the score is merely a support for his memory, not a fetter on his thought." The same writer in another place quotes von Bülow as dividing conductors into "those who have

* Weingartner. *On Conducting*, p. 43.

their heads in the score, and those who have the score in their heads"!

Study the individual voice parts, so as to find out so far as possible beforehand where the difficult spots are and mark these with blue pencil, so that when you want to drill on these places, you may be able to put your finger on them quickly. It is very easy to lose the attention of your performers by delay in finding the place which you want them to practise. It is a good plan, also, to mark with blue pencil some of the more important *dynamic* and *tempo* changes so that these may be obvious to the eye when you are standing several feet from the desk.

Decide beforehand upon some plan of studying each composition, and if a number of works are to be taken up at any given rehearsal, think over in advance the order in which they are to be studied. In brief, make a plan for each rehearsal, writing it out if necessary, and thus avoid wasting time in deciding what is to be done.

In case you are a choir director, learn also to plan your services weeks or even months in advance,* and then keep working toward the complete carrying out of your plan by familiarizing your musicians with the material as far in advance of the public performance as possible. In this way the music is *absorbed*, as it were, and the singers and players are much more apt to feel at ease in performing it than when it has been taken up at only one or two rehearsals.

DISCIPLINE IN THE REHEARSAL — It is impossible to conduct well unless you have the absolute attention of every singer or player. Hence the discipline at all rehearsals must be rather strict and the performers must be trained to keep their eyes on you practically all the time. (In the case of choral music, it would be well to have a great deal more of it entirely

---

* The complete list of works to be given by leading symphony orchestras during the entire season is usually decided upon during the preceding summer, and somewhat the same procedure might profitably be followed with a church choir or an amateur orchestra.

committed to memory so that at the performance the
singers might be enabled to give the conductor their
absolute attention.) You have a perfect right to demand
that all shall work industriously during every working
minute of the rehearsal hour and that there shall be no
whispering or fooling whatsoever, either while you are
giving directions, or while you are conducting. If you
are unfortunate enough to have in your organization
certain individuals who do not attend to the work in
hand even after a private admonition, it will be far better
to drop them from the organization, for they are bound
to do more harm than good if they are retained. On the
other hand, you will recognize the temptation to whisper
which the performer feels while you are giving a long-
winded explanation of some pet theory of yours, and you
will accordingly cut down the amount of talking you do to
the minimum. A good rule to follow is this: *"Talk little
at the rehearsal, but when you do talk, be sure that every one
listens."* Keep your performers so busy that they will
have no time to think about anything but the work in
hand. Plan plenty of work so as to be able to keep things
moving through the entire hour. Better a rehearsal
conducted in this way and only one hour long, than a
slow-moving, boresome affair, two hours in length. If
the tax of such concentrated attention is too severe to
be kept up constantly for an entire hour, plan to have
a five-minute intermission when everyone may talk and
laugh and thus relax. The author has found that with
a body of amateur singers, a ninety-minute rehearsal,
with a five- to seven-minute intermission in the middle,
works very well indeed.

BEGINNING THE   Do not shout at your chorus or
REHEARSAL   orchestra if the members are noisy.
                Wait until the noise subsides en-
tirely before you begin to speak, and address them in a
quiet, dignified, authoritative way when you do begin.

Unless you have some pointed remark to make about the rendition of the music, it is far better to give merely the place of beginning without making any remarks at all. Securing quiet by a prolonged rapping with the baton is a sign of weak discipline. Do not rap at all until the music is distributed, the accompanist in his place and ready to begin, your score open, and until you know exactly what you are going to do first. Then let just a slight tap or two suffice to notify everyone that the rehearsal is to begin at once.

LEARNING DIFFICULT PASSAGES In drilling on a difficult passage, it is usually better to stop at the actual spot where the mistake occurs than to go on to the end and then turn back. Find the exact spot that is causing trouble and "reduce the area of correction to its narrowest limits," as one writer * states it. It is to be noted that merely one repetition of such a passage is usually of little avail. *It must be gone over enough times to fix the correct method of rendition in mind and muscle as a habit.* If a section sings a certain passage incorrectly twice and then correctly only once, the chances are that the fourth time will be like the first two rather than like the third. The purpose of drilling on such a passage is to eradicate the wrong impression entirely and substitute for it an entirely new habit at that point. After learning a difficult tonal or rhythmic phrase in this way, be sure to fit it into its environment before assuming that it has been finally mastered. The difficulty in such passages often consists not in performing the intervals or rhythms in isolation, but in doing them while the other parts are going on.

LOCATE DIFFICULT SPOTS QUICKLY In directing attention to some particular place in the score about which you wish to speak, give the details of your direction always in the same order, *viz.:*

* Richardson, *The Choir-trainer's Art*, p. 156.

(1) page, (2) score (or *brace* if you prefer), (3) measure, (4) beat. Thus *e.g.*, "Page 47, second score, fourth measure, beginning with the second beat." Give the direction slowly and very distinctly, and then do not repeat it; *i.e.*, get your musicians into the habit of listening to you the first time you say a thing instead of the second or third. Carrying out this plan may result in confusing unpreparedness on the part of your singers or players for a time or two, but if the plan is adhered to consistently they will very soon learn to listen to your first announcement—and you will save a large amount of both time and energy.

REHEARSAL LETTERS
AND NUMBERS

Ensemble music is frequently supplied with *rehearsal letters* or *numbers*, these enabling the performers to locate a passage very quickly. When not printed in the score, it will often be a saving of time for the conductor to insert such letters or numbers in his own copy of the music in advance of the first rehearsal, asking the members to insert the marks in their music as he dictates their location by page and score, or by counting measures in the case of orchestra music. These letters or numbers are best inserted with soft red or blue pencil.

THE "WHOLE METHOD"
OF LEARNING

When a new composition is to be taken up, go through it as a whole a few times, so as to give everyone a general idea of its content and of the connection and relation of its parts. After this, begin to work at the difficult spots that you have found, then when it begins to go fairly well, work definitely for expressive rendition. You will of course not expect ordinary performers to go through the composition the first time in a very artistic fashion. If they keep going and do not make too many mistakes, they will have done all that non-professionals should be expected to do.

Psychologists have found as the result of careful investigation that the "whole method" of study is much to be preferred to what might be termed the "part method," because of the fact that a much clearer and closer association between parts is thus formed, and there is no doubt but that this point applies very forcibly to the study of music. In an interview published in the *New York World* in June, 1916, Harold Bauer writes as follows about this matter as related to piano music:

Now, in taking up a new work for the piano, the child could and should play right through every page from beginning to end for the purpose of obtaining a definite first impression of the whole. A mess would probably be made of it technically, but no matter. He would gradually discover just where the places were that required technical smoothing, and then by playing them over slowly these spots would be technically strengthened. By the time the composition was thoroughly learned the technique would be thoroughly acquired, too. Obtaining first a perfect mental picture of the whole, and afterward working out the details, is better than learning a work by starting with the details before gaining a broad impression of the composition as a whole.

This method of studying musical compositions is especially important from the standpoint of *expression*. In many an instance, the source of wrong interpretation (or of no interpretation at all) may be traced directly to a method of studying the composition which has not impressed the singers or players with its essential meaning and spirit, and with the significance of the various details in relation to the plan of the work as a whole. This is particularly true of choral compositions, and in taking up such works, it may often be well for the conductor to read aloud the entire text of the chorus that is being studied in order that the attention of the singers may be focused for a few moments upon the imagery conveyed by the words. Such attention is frequently impossible while singing, because the minds of the singers are intent upon the beauty or difficulty of the purely musical aspects of the composition, and thus the so-called "expression" becomes merely a blind and uninspired obedience to certain marks like *piano*, *forte*, and *ritardando*—the real spirit of interpretation being entirely absent.

DISTRIBUTING AND CARING FOR THE MUSIC   Have the distribution and care of music so systematized that there will be neither confusion nor waste of time in this part of the rehearsal. In a professional organization there will of course be a salaried librarian to see to such work, but it is entirely possible to secure somewhat the same kind of results in an amateur body by having two or three members elected or appointed for the task, these persons serving either entirely without salary or being paid a purely nominal sum. These librarians will then be expected to take the responsibility of marking new music, of distributing and collecting it at such times as may be agreed upon by librarian and conductor, and of caring for it at concerts or at any other time when it is to be used.

It will be the duty also of the head librarian to keep a record of all music loaned or rented, and to see that it is returned in good condition. It would be well too if he kept a card index, showing just what music is owned by the organization, the number of copies of each selection, the price, the publisher, the date when purchased, *et cetera*. Ask the librarians to come five or ten minutes before the beginning of the rehearsal, and make it your business to provide one of them with a slip having upon it the names or numbers of all the selections to be used at that particular rehearsal. Keeping the music in covers or in separate compartments of a cabinet, one of which will hold all of the copies of a single selection, and having these arranged alphabetically or numerically, will considerably facilitate matters for both you and the librarians. Do not think it beneath your dignity to investigate the number of copies of any composition that you are planning to use, and when there are not enough to supply each singer in the chorus and each desk in the orchestra with a copy, to see to it that more music is ordered. It is impossible to rehearse efficiently if the singers in a chorus have to use a part of their energy in trying to read music from a book or sheet held by some one else, or if the players in an orchestra are straining their eyes because three or four instead of two are reading from a single desk.

It will be convenient for the conductor to possess a file containing a copy of each number in the library at his home or studio, each copy being marked "conductor's copy." In this way, the director will always be assured of having the same music, and will feel that it is worth while to mark it in such a way as to make it more useful in both rehearsal and performance.

COUNTING ALOUD, TAPPING, AND SINGING WITH THE CHORUS — Do not make the mistake of counting or tapping on the desk constantly during the rehearsal. You may think you are strengthening the rhythm, but as a matter of fact, you are actually weakening it, for in this way you take away from the performers the necessity of individual muscular response to the pulse, and at the performance (when you cannot, of course, count or tap) the rhythm is very likely to be flabby and uncertain. Singing with the chorus is another mistake against which the amateur should be warned. The director not only cannot detect errors and make intelligent criticisms if he sings with the chorus, but will make the members dependent upon his voice instead of compelling them to form the habit of watching him. The only exception to this principle is in teaching new music to a choir composed of very poor readers, in which case it is sometimes much easier to teach a difficult phrase by imitation. Even here, however, it is almost as well to have the organ give the correct tones. In leading community singing, the conductor will of course sing with the crowd, for here he is striving for quite a different sort of effect.

VENTILATION   See to it that the practice room is well ventilated, especially for a chorus rehearsal. Plenty of fresh air will not only enable your chorus to sing with better intonation, but will allow them to sing for a longer period without fatigue. (We are tempted to add a corollary to this proposition: namely, that sleepy congregations are not always due to poor preaching, as is generally supposed, but are as frequently the result of a combination of fairly good preaching and a badly ventilated auditorium!)

A CAPPELLA REHEARSING   In directing a chorus rehearsal, have your singers study without accompaniment much of the time. The organ "covers a multitude of sins" and practising without it will not only enable you to discover weaknesses of all sorts but will help the singers themselves enormously by making them more independent, improving the intonation, and compelling them to make cleaner and more definite attacks and releases.

THE VALUE OF A SENSE OF HUMOR   Finally, in concluding both this chapter and the book as a whole, let us commend once more to the conductor that he cultivate "the saving grace of humor." This quality has already been commented on somewhat at length in an earlier chapter (see p. 8), but it is in the rehearsal period that it is most needed, and the conductor who is fortunate enough to be able to laugh a little when annoyances interrupt or disrupt his plans instead of snarling, will not only hold the members of the organization together for a longer time, because of their cordial personal attitude toward him, but will find himself much less fatigued at the end of the rehearsal;

for nothing drains one's vitality so rapidly as scolding. A bit of humorous repartee, then, especially in response to the complaints of some lazy or grouchy performer; the ability to meet accidental mishaps without anger; even a humorous anecdote to relieve the strain of a taxing rehearsal—all these are to be highly recommended as means of oiling the machinery of the rehearsal and making it run smoothly.

But of course, even humor can be overdone. So we shall close by quoting the Greek motto, "Nothing too much," which will be found to apply equally well to many other activities recommended in the foregoing pages.

APPENDIX A

Reference List

I. GENERAL:

Berlioz, *The Orchestral Conductor*. A short treatise full of practical suggestions. It is found in the back of the author's well-known volume on *Orchestration*.

Weingartner, *On Conducting*. A small volume of about seventy-five pages, but containing excellent material for both amateur and professional.

Schroeder, *Handbook of Conducting*. A practical little book from the standpoint of both orchestral and operatic directing.

Wagner, *On Conducting*. A short treatise that every professional conductor will wish to read, but not of much value to the amateur.

Mees, *Choirs and Choral Music*. A well-written account of the history of choral music from the time of the Hebrews and Greeks down to the present, containing also an excellent chapter on the Chorus Conductor.

Grove, *Dictionary of Music and Musicians* (article, Conducting).

Henderson, *What Is Good Music?* (chapters XIII and XVII).

Krehbiel, *How to Listen to Music* (chapter VIII).

II. INTERPRETATION:

Coward, *Choral Technique and Interpretation*. One of the few really significant books on conducting. The author gives in a clear and practical way the principles on which his own successful work as a choral conductor was based.

Matthay, *Musical Interpretation*. A book for the musician in general, rather than for the conductor specifically; an excellent treatise and one that all musicians should read.

III. THE ORCHESTRA:

Lavignac, *Music and Musicians* (chapter II).

Mason, *The Orchestral Instruments and What They Do*.

Corder, *The Orchestra and How to Write for It*.

Prout, *The Orchestra* (two volumes).

Kling, *Modern Orchestration and Instrumentation*.

Henderson, *The Orchestra and Orchestral Music;* contains two chapters (XII and XIII) on the Orchestral Conductor that will be of great interest to the amateur.

Mason (Editor), *The Art of Music* (Vol. VIII).

Stoeving, *The Art of Violin Bowing.*

Forsyth, *Orchestration.* A particularly good book both for professional and amateur, as it gives many illustrations and treats the various instruments from an historical as well as a practical standpoint

Widor, *The Modern Orchestra.*

IV. THE CHURCH CHOIR:

Curwen, *Studies in Worship Music* (two volumes).

Dickinson, *Music in the History of the Western Church.*

Helmore, *Primer of Plainsong.*

Pratt, *Musical Ministries in the Church.*

V. THE BOY CHOIR:

Bates, *Voice Culture for Children.*

Brown and Behnke, *The Child Voice.*

Howard, *The Child Voice in Singing.*

Johnson, *The Training of Boys' Voices.*

Richardson, *The Choir Trainer's Art.*

Stubbs, *Practical Hints on Boy Choir Training.*

VI. VOICE TRAINING:

Ffrangçon-Davies, *The Singing of the Future.*

Fillebrown, *Resonance in Singing and Speaking.*

Greene, *Interpretation in Song.*

Henderson, *The Art of the Singer.*

Russell, *English Diction for Singers and Speakers.*

Withrow, *Some Staccato Notes for Singers.*

VII. MISCELLANEOUS:

Hamilton, *Outlines of Music History.*

Hamilton, *Sound and Its Relation to Music.*

VIII. RECENT PUBLICATIONS:

Earhart, *The Eloquent Baton.*

Carse, *Orchestral Conducting.*

Stoessel, *Technic of the Baton.*

APPENDIX B

HAYDN—SYMPHONY N⁰3
"Surprise" Symphony

Score of Second Movement

INDEX